This book is dedicated to the educators
who have inspired us and to the students
who have challenged us as educators.

Contents

Activity Finder   vi

Preface   x

Acknowledgments   xii

Introduction   xiii

CHAPTER **1**

Maximum Learning for All 1

Establish Student Expectations 2

Assess Yourself 3

Assess Your Students 4

Maximize Learning Time 5

Explain and Enforce Department Procedures 5

Establish Class Management Protocols 8

Get Off to a Good Start 11

Activities 18

CHAPTER **2**

Fitness Made Fun 41

Incentives 42

Success and Fun for All 44

Structuring Lessons 47

Putting It Together 47

Activities 52

CHAPTER **3**

Social Skills Development 77

Elements of a Successful Social Skills Curriculum 78

Developing the Curriculum 80

Activities 83

MAXIMUM
Middle School
Physical Education

Mary Hirt

California State University, Northridge

Irene Ramos

University of California, Los Angeles

Human Kinetics

Library of Congress Cataloging-in-Publication Data

Hirt, Mary, 1962-
  Maximum middle school physical education / Mary Hirt, Irene Ramos.
    p. cm.
  Includes bibliographical references.
  ISBN-13: 978-0-7360-5779-0 (soft cover)
  ISBN-10: 0-7360-5779-X (soft cover)
  1. Physical education and training--Study and teaching (Middle school)--United States. 2. Lesson
planning--United States. I. Ramos, Irene, 1957- II. Title.
  GV223.H55 2008
  613.7071'2--dc22

                              2007041050
ISBN-10: 0-7360-5779-X
ISBN-13: 978-0-7360-5779-0

The Web addresses cited in this text were current as of January 2008, unless otherwise noted.

Acquisitions Editor: Bonnie Pettifor Vreeman; **Developmental Editor:** Ray Vallese; **Assistant Editor:** Derek Campbell; **Copyeditor:** Alisha Jeddeloh; **Proofreader:** Julie Marx Goodreau; **Permission Manager:** Dalene Reeder; **Graphic Designer:** Fred Starbird; **Graphic Artist:** Dawn Sills; **Cover Designer:** Keith Blomberg; **Photographer (cover):** Mary Hirt; **Photographer (interior):** Courtesy of Mary Hirt, unless otherwise noted; © Human Kinetics, pp. 77, 111, 131, and 159; **Photo Asset Manager:** Laura Fitch; **Photo Office Assistant:** Jason Allen; **Art Manager:** Kelly Hendren; **Associate Art Manager:** Alan L. Wilborn; **Illustrator:** Lineworks, Inc.; **Printer:** Versa Press

Printed in the United States of America

10 9 8 7 6 5 4 3 2 1

Human Kinetics
Web site: www.HumanKinetics.com

United States: Human Kinetics
P.O. Box 5076
Champaign, IL 61825-5076
800-747-4457
e-mail: humank@hkusa.com

Canada: Human Kinetics
475 Devonshire Road Unit 100
Windsor, ON N8Y 2L5
800-465-7301 (in Canada only)
e-mail: info@hkcanada.com

Europe: Human Kinetics
107 Bradford Road
Stanningley
Leeds LS28 6AT, United Kingdom
+44 (0) 113 255 5665
e-mail: hk@hkeurope.com

Australia: Human Kinetics
57A Price Avenue
Lower Mitcham, South Australia 5062
08 8372 0999
e-mail: info@hkaustralia.com

New Zealand: Human Kinetics
Division of Sports Distributors NZ Ltd.
P.O. Box 300 226 Albany
North Shore City
Auckland
0064 9 448 1207
e-mail: info@humankinetics.co.nz

CHAPTER **4**

Student-Centered Learning **111**

Laying the Foundation 112

Unit 1: Juggling 113

Unit 2: Circus Tricks 118

Unit 3: Tossing, Throwing, Catching, and Striking 124

Unit 4: Foot Skills 128

Summary 130

CHAPTER **5**

Sequence Learning **131**

Unit 1: Using Grids in Team Sport 132

Unit 2: Gladiator Games 142

Unit 3: Rhythm and Dance 147

CHAPTER **6**

Promoting Your Program **155**

Address the Three Circles of Influence 156

Build the Curriculum 157

Spread the Word 159

Find Support 160

References and Resources   163

About the Authors   164

How to Use the CD-ROM   165

Activity Finder

Activity	Category	Page number
Affirmation Circle	Team initiative	30
All Aboard	Team initiative	27
Back to Back	Sequence learning (gladiator games)	145
Balance Tag	Fitness made fun (full game)	64
Ball Taps	Fitness made fun (individual)	48
Ball Wrestling	Sequence learning (gladiator games)	145
Battling Combats	Sequence learning (gladiator games)	145
Beam-Out	Social skills	92
Beehives	Fitness made fun (full game)	69
Before-Class Challenges	Class management	11
Boardroom	Social skills	94
Breakthrough	Sequence learning (gladiator games)	146
Bull-Ring Transport	Social skills	102
Canoe Race	Social skills	102
Can Pass	Fitness made fun (group)	50
Card Ranking	Team initiative	31
Cat and Mouse	Fitness made fun (full game)	72
Chicken–Tire Tag	Fitness made fun (full game)	62
Circus Tricks	Student-centered learning	118
Classroom Temperature	Team initiative	32
Clothespin Tag	Fitness made fun (full game)	60
Collective Tally	Team initiative	33
Compass	Social skills	85
Cone Savers	Fitness made fun (full game)	57
Courtesy Tag	Team initiative	36
Crash	Sequence learning (movement steps)	152
Data Processing	Social skills	83
Design Your Own Logo	Icebreaker activity	14
Design Your Own Totem Pole	Icebreaker activity	14
Dice Push-Ups	Fitness made fun (partner)	49
Diminishing Circle	Social skills	103
Dog Bone	Sequence learning (gladiator games)	144
Dome Balance	Social skills	104
Don't Touch Me	Social skills	84
Dowel Exchange	Social skills	108

Activity	Category	Page number
Dutch Relay	Social skills	88
Eagle's Nest	Team initiative	28
Eurofoam Mania	Fitness made fun (full game)	61
Finger Trap	Team initiative	22
Fire Escape	Social skills	98
Fitness Scrabble	Fitness made fun (full game)	74
Flag Grab	Sequence learning (gladiator games)	145
Foot-Pass Train	Fitness made fun (group)	56
Foot Skills	Student-centered learning	128
Form a Letter	Social skills	104
Four Corners	Fitness made fun	52
Four-Letter Word	Team initiative	34
Freeze and Thaw	Social skills	100
Fruits of Your Labor	Team initiative	20
Group Get-Up	Team initiative	25
Half-Tennis-Ball Elbow Snatch	Team initiative	32
Half the Feet	Team initiative	38
Healthy Helpfuls	Reinforcing positive behaviors	10
Hi, How Are You? Gotta Go	Team initiative	35
Hog Call	Social skills	101
Hold 'Em Back	Sequence learning (gladiator games)	144
Houdini Hoops	Social skills	109
How Can I Help You Crew	Reinforcing positive behaviors	10
Hula Hoop Relay	Social skills	94
Hula-Hula	Team initiative	23
Juggling	Student-centered learning	113
Jump Rope	Sequence learning (movement steps)	152
Jurassic Planet	Social skills	107
Knights Unite	Fitness made fun (full game)	68
Knock It Off	Social skills	107
Krazy Kones	Fitness made fun (full game)	73
Leading the Passer	Sequence learning (grids in team sports)	136
Leg Wrestling	Sequence learning (gladiator games)	146
The Lottery	Class management	9
Math Face-Off	Team initiative	38
Math on the Move	Fitness made fun	53
Minefield	Social skills	95
Mingle	Team initiative	19
Monarchy Versus Anarchy	Fitness made fun (full game)	72
Mosquito Tag	Fitness made fun (full game)	67

(continued)

(continued)

Activity	Category	Page number
Moving to Open Space	Sequence learning (grids in team sports)	134
Moving With the Ball	Sequence learning (grids in team sports)	141
Moving Without the Ball	Sequence learning (grids in team sports)	137
My Last Breath	Fitness made fun (full game)	75
Mystical Wave	Team initiative	39
Neat Puzzle	Social skills	96
No-Rope Tug	Sequence learning (gladiator games)	146
Observation Deck	Team initiative	18
Paper Dance	Sequence learning (movement steps)	148
Partner Ball Exchange	Fitness made fun (partner)	54
Partner Get-Up	Team initiative	24
Partner Pull	Social skills	100
Partner Squat and Push-Up	Fitness made fun (partner)	55
Pass the Fat Tag	Fitness made fun (full game)	66
Pipeline	Team initiative	29
Playing Defense	Sequence learning (grids in team sports)	138
Pop or Be Popped	Fitness made fun (full game)	63
Power Ball	Sequence learning (gladiator games)	146
Protect Your Turf	Social skills	97
Pulse	Team initiative	23
Push-Up Ball Touches	Fitness made fun (individual)	48
Push-Up Hockey or Soccer	Fitness made fun (partner)	49
Push-Up Pull	Sequence learning (gladiator games)	145
Push-Up Snatch	Fitness made fun (partner)	49
Push-Up Toss	Fitness made fun (partner)	49
Push-Up Toss Up and Over	Fitness made fun (partner)	49
Put-Ups	Reinforcing positive behaviors	10
Random Acts of Kindness	Class management	9
Random Count	Team initiative	37
River Crossing	Social skills	89
Rock, Paper, Scissors	Team initiative	21
Roll Around	Fitness made fun (individual)	48
Rope Jousting	Sequence learning (gladiator games)	144
Roundup	Fitness made fun (full game)	60
Scrum Soccer	Social skills	93
Shark Attack	Social skills	91
Shark Bait	Team initiative	28
Short Circuits	Fitness made fun (group)	50
Smokers Tag	Fitness made fun (full game)	65
Snatch and Grab	Fitness made fun (partner)	49

Activity	Category	Page number
Speed Count	Social skills	98
Spin Tag	Fitness made fun (full game)	62
Squash Balls	Social skills	106
Star Gate	Social skills	87
Stock Market	Team initiative	34
Student Bingo	Icebreaker activity	14
Stump Jump	Social skills	99
Sumo Master	Sequence learning (gladiator games)	144
Tanks and Commanders	Social skills	86
Tarp Magic	Social skills	105
Teeter-Totter Tag	Fitness made fun (full game)	66
Three Hs	Reinforcing positive behaviors	10
Three-Person Challenge	Fitness made fun (partner)	49
Thumb Wrestling	Team initiative	36
Tinikling	Sequence learning (movement steps)	148
Tire Run	Fitness made fun (full game)	59
Toe Tag	Social skills	83
Tossing, Throwing, Catching, and Striking	Student-centered learning	124
Towel Tug	Sequence learning (gladiator games)	146
Traffic Jam	Social skills	90
Triangle Tag	Social skills	86
Tricky Triangle	Social skills	91
Trio Tag	Fitness made fun (full game)	64
Two-Ball Challenge	Fitness made fun (full game)	70
Ultimate Hockey or Soccer	Fitness made fun (full game)	71
Walk-a-Hula	Social skills	87
Yellow Brick Road Scavenger Hunt	Icebreaker activity	14

Preface

Welcome to *Maximum Middle School Physical Education.* This book and its CD-ROM are designed for immediate practical use by physical educators. More importantly, they are designed to help you create an environment where students are active and excited and enjoy physical education. In maximum physical education, students can't wait to participate and share their experiences with friends and family. Maximum physical education is more than lesson plans, assessment sheets, and fitness and psychomotor development—it's about developing health and wellness through joyful movement.

Throughout the book, we have chosen to write examples in first person and refer to Lincoln Middle School as a site where many lessons were learned. Even though the book is authored by two people, the single voice for us adds clarity to the message.

About MOOMBA

Health and wellness is not just what we do, it's who we are. It's an attitude, a way of being and interacting with the world around us. As physical educators, we teach students to think in a manner that nourishes their development. In order for students to become physically educated, they must become mentally fit. This attitude will then be reflected in how they live—what they do will show who they are.

This outlook can be characterized with the acronym *MOOMBA,* or "My only obstacle must be attitude." If we teach students how to empower themselves, we'll unleash a beautiful, creative force that can make this world a better place. Empowerment through wellness will result in communities filled with respect, care, and integrity. MOOMBA teaches us that the only obstacle is ourselves. As teachers, we have the power to create a nurturing environment that fosters students' love for movement. We are entrusted with their care and must assume this responsibility with diligence.

As a little girl, I would sit for hours admiring the fish in my parents' aquarium. The colors, gracefulness, and lively interaction among the fish fascinated me. In 2004, I installed a koi pond in my backyard. I spent many hours reading everything I could about pH levels, temperatures, habitats, and water filtering systems. I interviewed experts and visited other ponds. I examined the koi and learned how to properly care for them. Finally, as I prepared to introduce the fish into the pond, it occurred to me how much they were relying on me to provide them with the necessary conditions for their survival. Their lives totally depended on my expertise and care. I controlled their environment. That's when I realized how responsible I was for their ability to not only survive but also thrive. This same principle is true in education. As a teacher, I control the environment of my classroom. I have the power to regulate the conditions for my students to learn and grow.

MOOMBA is the theme that runs throughout this book. It is essential to creating a learning environment where all students feel respected, valued, and loved. My hope is that it will not only become part of your program but will become part of your life as well. When we can all adopt an attitude of health and wellness, we will live in a world where respect for others and self is central to all we do. MOOMBA is that attitude.

About This Book

Maximum Middle School Physical Education was created to provide a framework for uniting all the good work you are doing. Throughout each physical experience you will find a thread that reinforces a love for life and self, as well as respect for others. The book and CD-ROM will support your efforts to create a learning environment in which all students experience success, become physically active, and incorporate movement in their lives because they love it.

The book is organized to first provide strategies for creating a learning environment that fosters a love for movement. It offers practical activities that you can immediately implement to teach students how to treat each other with respect, have the courage to try new tasks, and support each other. Then you can choose from a variety of activities that develop fitness and skills, engage students, and include everyone.

The book is organized in six distinct chapters:

- Chapter 1: Maximum Learning for All provides practical ways to start the year off right by establishing clear expectations for student behaviors that support student learning.

- Chapter 2: Fitness Made Fun provides you with many activities that develop fitness but are fun and engaging for students.

- Chapter 3: Social Skills Development addresses a standard that usually is unspoken or not articulated well to students. Here we specifically address issues of respect, responsibility, teamwork, communication, leadership, and conflict resolution. We introduce ways to promote and sustain positive social interactions with students through activities and games.

- Chapter 4: Student-Centered Learning is about creating the independent learner and the teacher as facilitator. Four complete units are provided that allow for the student to explore movement in a purposeful, structured setting.

- Chapter 5: Sequence Learning provides movement experiences that build on one another. These building blocks for student learning provide a model for developing lessons that reinforce previous learning and build students' skills and confidence.

- Chapter 6: Promoting Your Program is all about how to find ways to continue to build a program that provides quality physical education experiences for students and their families.

Because we believe it is important to support the work outlined in the book, a CD-ROM is included that contains assessment sheets, task cards, posters, instructional diagrams, and recognition sheets to get you started. Just look for the thumbnails of the support materials, and you'll know that materials are ready for you to use on the CD-ROM. (See page 165 for technical details on using the CD-ROM.)

Acknowledgments

We would like to recognize John Hichwa, Jim Clemmensen, Jean Flemion, Kristen Okura, and Ilene Straus. Your passion for educational excellence is contagious, and your work guided us to meet the needs of every child that entered through our gym doors. We are thankful for the enthusiasm, patience, and wisdom you have shared with us over the years.

We would like to thank the students we have worked with over the years who have challenged us as teachers. You pushed our teaching to reflect the best practices in education. Many of the activities contained in this book are there because of you.

Finally, we would like to thank our families, who have supported us throughout this process.

MOOMBA! My Only Obstacle Must Be Attitude

Move or go around the obstacles that are in your way of attaining your goals.

Introduction

Through years of trying to engage students in our lessons and classrooms, we have discovered that the way we approach students makes all the difference. *Maximum Middle School Physical Education* is designed to help you create a special environment where all students feel that they matter. The acronym *MOOMBA*, meaning "My only obstacle must be attitude," is about creating that space. Having enthusiasm for movement, self, and others is contagious. We have the ability to create such a space for our students if we are attuned to our actions and our attitudes.

This book is not about analyzing movement skills; many excellent physical educators have done a wonderful job of breaking down skills and discussing how to help students acquire them. Instead, this book is about making sure students practice those skills in an environment that is fun, safe, and supportive. The key concept is that before any activity in this book can be successful, it must take place in an environment that makes movement a joyful part of every student's life. By modeling behaviors, reinforcing those behaviors, communicating clear expectations, and teaching skills through guided work, you can create a learning environment that fosters student learning.

Beliefs and Practices

In the 1990s, a popular trend among businesses was creating a mission statement. This usually involved company executives spending long hours in a room with a consultant, talking about what the mission statement should be. Invariably, they'd come up with something such as, "Committed to excellence and customer service." Their work was proudly displayed in an oak or mahogany frame in the company lunchroom, only to gather dust.

A mission statement as general as "Committed to excellence and customer service" gives no picture of what that ideal would look like in practice. For some, it might mean offering the best price, whereas for others, it might mean providing the best products. In order for a program to be effective in attaining its goals, everyone responsible for delivering a service must agree on what that service should look like, make a personal commitment to practice behaviors that serve that goal, and develop group accountability to make the ideal into a reality.

A few companies understand the value of committing to a set of core beliefs that transcend all that is done within the organization. Apple, Starbucks, and Southwest Airlines are just three examples of companies with a commitment to make their mission statement a reality. Let's take a closer look at Starbucks, which was founded on the ideal of offering the best and freshest coffee on the market. The Starbucks mission statement reads as follows:

Establish Starbucks as the premier purveyor of the finest coffee in the world while maintaining our uncompromising principles while we grow.

The following six guiding principles will help us measure the appropriateness of our decisions:

- Provide a great work environment and treat each other with respect and dignity.
- Embrace diversity as an essential component in the way we do business.

- Apply the highest standards of excellence to the purchasing, roasting, and fresh delivery of our coffee.
- Develop enthusiastically satisfied customers all of the time.
- Contribute positively to our communities and our environment.
- Recognize that profitability is essential to our future success.

The success of Starbucks can be seen while driving by any of their stores early in the morning. Lines of people form before the doors open, waiting to purchase coffee that they could easily make at home. Instead they prefer the Starbucks experience of having a barista fill their mugs with coffee that is made especially for them. The Starbucks mission statement lives through their stores. In the same way, quality physical education must be evident in everything that we do.

What does quality physical education look like, and how can teachers make sure every student experiences it? The end result will be lines of children waiting for the locker rooms to open because they are so excited for the movement experience to come. To achieve this, physical educators need facilitators who are willing to help them understand what their true beliefs are as demonstrated in their actual practices. What teachers do in the classroom each day reveals their belief system. Is there a gap between what you believe to be best practices and your daily work? If so, then you need to develop a plan of improvement to create a quality physical education experience for all.

Four Steps to Quality Physical Education

Every school can develop a quality physical education program. It starts with assessing your personal beliefs, defining best practices, and translating that belief into practice each day. Too many times, leaders act more as scouts, going into the wild and cutting their own paths. It's tempting to go it alone because you can do what you want, when you want, and how you want it done. You may be able to quickly accomplish your personal goals, and it may be a lot more fun; however, it does not create quality physical education for every child. To create a quality physical education program, each person within the department must assess the team's beliefs, determine the best way to achieve those objectives, commit to demonstrating the values in practice, and hold each other accountable for living the core beliefs.

Step 1: Assess Your Operational Beliefs

Thoughts and intention are important, but it is practice that reveals beliefs. There usually are common beliefs that people can easily agree upon, such as the belief that every child should participate in daily physical activity. The key, however, is how well this belief statement translates into actual practice. How do teachers respond to a child who is not dressed appropriately for physical activity, is ill, or is misbehaving? Their response reveals their operational beliefs, or their true beliefs about daily participation.

What must teachers do to adhere to the core belief that every child should participate in daily physical activity? This is where the real work begins. Following is an example of how the belief in daily participation translates into practice.

If we believe all students should participate on a daily basis, we must commit to making this belief a reality. Therefore, we will provide loaners for students who are not dressed to participate in physical education, and we will modify activities so students with various skill levels and disabilities can fully participate in all activities.

Compare your program with your state curriculum standards or use the program assessment tool provided by the National Association for Sport and Physical Education (NASPE) (1998). Learn what a quality program looks like and determine what beliefs dominate practices in your program. Do the curriculum and instruction in your department reflect appropriate practices? What collective belief is the most important to department members? Be honest with yourself and have the courage to reveal true practices and select areas of growth to improve your program.

What kind of role model will you be for your students?

Step 2: Define Your Goal

At this point, it is critical to select a manageable goal. The change process demands careful communication with students, parents, coworkers, and the school administration. For change to be successful, people who are affected by the change must understand its value and support it.

Collectively rate what is most important to your department compared with outstanding practices in physical education. Your group will likely come up with several main beliefs. Rank them in importance and develop a multiyear plan to accomplish them one at a time. Take small steps but take the steps together, committed to moving in the same direction. Remind yourselves often why you are doing what you are doing.

For example, you might adopt some of the following values:

- Physical education will instill a love of movement in all children.
- Students will work cooperatively in a respectful manner.
- All students will participate on a daily basis.
- Students will experience success.

Step 3: Commit to the Mission Statement

Develop a mission statement expressing the values to which everyone will commit. Remember, the mission statement creates a standard that all practices can be evaluated against. For example, consider the statement, "Students will work cooperatively in a respectful manner." How might middle school physical education staff ensure that this belief is actualized in daily practice? Perhaps the staff could

- offer group initiatives or lessons that teach students how to be respectful,
- provide activities where students can practice respectful behavior,
- hold students and staff accountable for demonstrating respectful behavior, and
- model respectful behavior for students.

A visitor to this middle school would see this belief reflected in teacher behavior. *Please* and *thank you* are common words spoken by the physical education staff toward students and each other, and social skills are regularly incorporated in the curriculum. Teachers use activities to develop particular social skills and take time within the lesson to model the skills toward students, provide opportunities for students to practice the skills, and reinforce the behavior throughout the year.

As you establish belief statements, be sure to provide specific examples of how each value can be seen and experienced by students and staff. It is important that they know exactly what behaviors are expected of them. What will the new behavior look like, what will it sound like, and how will they know they were successful? In other words, what behaviors will you expect to see in students because of your teaching?

Step 4: Be Responsible and Accountable

Finally, everyone must be responsible for putting beliefs into practice. All teachers must be willing to be open with their classroom practices and share success stories as well as failures. Only then can common core beliefs become the department way.

At Lincoln Middle School, where I have taught for more than 15 years, there is a strong commitment to the Lincoln Way. Lincoln Middle School has been recognized as a California Distinguished School, a National Blue Ribbon School, and a Disney Spotlight School. In addition, renowned educator Ted Sizer used Lincoln Middle School as an example of strong school culture in *Horace's Hope* (1996) because the Lincoln Way is taught to newcomers and everything about the school embodies it.

A professional standard of practices has been established at the school, and staff understand its importance to student achievement. Teachers have become educational leaders and are courageous enough to challenge practices that are incongruent with their professional belief in best practices. Additionally, each staff member has made a personal commitment to hold one another accountable to practicing the standard each day, in each lesson, with each child. If teachers can hold one another accountable to agreed standards, the quality of the educational experience for students and staff reaches its highest form.

Developing a Curriculum

Physical activity is critical to the development and maintenance of health and wellness. The goal of physical education is to develop physically educated people who have the knowledge, skills, and confidence to enjoy a lifetime of physical activity. Review your curriculum to see what you must include, revise, or exclude to meet your state and national standards.

Scope and Sequence

Use the building blocks of scope and sequence to develop a curriculum that builds on previous learning. *Scope* refers to what is taught to students. This includes a list of activities students will experience in a school year. What activities will students be exposed to in sixth grade versus eighth grade? The scope of the curriculum allows educators to see if there is a balance of movement experiences and to identify units that should be included to meet national and state standards in physical education. For example, rhythm and dance are commonly included in many state standards, which means teachers must ensure that students are exposed to this movement experience during their educational experience.

Sequence refers to the order in which skills are taught. A good curriculum builds on previous learning. When creating lessons to teach skills, consider when the skills will be taught and what will follow that instruction. Many educators' first reaction is to examine a particular unit, such as basketball, and build a foundation of learning that slowly moves to more complex skills. For example, a teacher might focus on ball handling before teaching shooting skills. But a better strategy is to examine the school year as a whole. What learning experiences are essential for students to master before they enter the basketball unit? The well-developed curriculum will sequence learning experiences that allow students to be skillful in movement without the ball before exposing them to activities requiring them to handle the ball.

An easy way to remember the difference between scope and sequence is to think of scope as horizontal teaching. As with a horizon, scope lets you see what is laid out before you. What will you cover while students are under your care? What topics or skills will you cover during the year? Sequence, on the other hand, is vertical teaching. What do students need to know in order to be successful in the next unit? Sequence builds a foundation for the next level of learning. Particular skills must be mastered in order to provide a strong foundation for more complex skills.

An example of a good scope and sequence for soccer would be to introduce a footbag unit before a soccer unit. Students thus develop eye–foot coordination in a setting that focuses solely on individual skills. Using a footbag as a primary building block before beginning a soccer unit makes it more likely that students will succeed in the program. This example illustrates how physical educators can incorporate units that build competency of movement before beginning a unit that requires a complex set of skills.

Guidelines for Best Practices

As you review your curriculum, here are some general guidelines for developing a scope and sequence that reflect best practices. First, ask yourself what students are expected to learn by the time they complete the unit, year, and program. Many state standards list what students should know, but it is important to ask yourself how that knowledge is demonstrated through student behavior. What standard of performance do you expect from students? How will you assess them? Physical educators who are committed to quality physical education ask these questions regularly with their colleagues and can provide evidence of student performance to evaluate whether students are indeed learning what is expected.

What are appropriate activities for different grade levels and students? Developing appropriate activities requires planning and constant evaluation of student performance. Understanding sequence and the fundamentals of movement allows educators to prepare activities where students build confidence in their skills and are willing to take risks with new skills. Because learning is a dynamic process that depends on the students, teachers must monitor student performance and identify times when teaching fails to bring about the desired result. This slight shift in responsibility for learning is crucial in creating a learning environment that allows the teacher to adjust to the demands of the learner. The focus shifts to ways to engage students and compel them to participate fully.

It is important to build professional relationships with other teachers in order to develop a curriculum that maximizes student and teacher performance. When two or more teachers discuss and share best practices, a synergy is created. To be successful in education and to build outstanding programs of instruction, teachers must be able to share what they have learned. There are many positive examples of best practices physical educators have developed through the years, so why go it alone?

Some states describe specific activities that are appropriate for each grade level, whereas others are more general. The key is to have a conversation with yourself that reveals any beliefs, biases, and judgments that may need revision in order to implement a quality physical education program. NASPE provides excellent documents to begin this process. The NASPE national standards for physical education (figure I.1; see also figure I.1 on the CD-ROM), the NASPE appropriate practices for middle school physical education, and the NASPE self-assessment tool all provide a strong foundation from which to begin. To learn more about quality physical education practices, visit the NASPE Web site at www.aahperd.org/naspe.

1. Demonstrates competency in motor skills and movement patterns needed to perform a variety of physical activities.

2. Demonstrates understanding of movement concepts, principles, strategies, and tactics as they apply to the learning and performance of physical activities.

3. Participates regularly in physical activity.

4. Achieves and maintains a health-enhancing level of physical fitness.

5. Exhibits responsible personal and social behavior that respects self and others in physical activity settings.

6. Values physical activity for health, enjoyment, challenge, self-expression, or social interaction.

FIGURE I.1 The NASPE national standards.

Reprinted from *Moving into the Future: National Standards for Physical Education,* Second Edition, with permission from the National Association for Sport and Physical Education (NASPE), 1900 Association Drive, Reston, VA 20191, USA.

The purpose of physical education is to develop lifetime health and wellness in each child, and this purpose has a unique place in education. Never before have so many children suffered from inactivity and poor diet. As physical educators, we have a duty to ensure our students are able to live life to its fullest. A lifelong pursuit of movement activities that bring enjoyment, social interaction, and physical health requires that students appreciate the benefits of daily physical activity. Therefore, as you examine your program and compare it with programs that are seen as exemplary, be willing to ask the following questions:

1. Are all students participating on a daily basis? Participation involves full engagement. Is time maximized so that all students are physically engaged as much as possible, benefiting from purposeful movement activities? If not, why? What are the obstacles that prevent them from engaging in the learning activity? How can you have more students on task, more often?

2. Is the learning environment respectful of everyone? All students have the right to participate in a learning environment where their contributions are valued and nurtured. Differentiated instruction that meets students at their level of performance and raises them to the next level is essential to creating a place where all students feel respected and are willing to take risks.

3. Are you providing a rich experience for students? During the middle school years, students should be exposed to a wide range of learning experiences, allowing them to develop a large repertoire of movement skills. From this broad base of rich movement experiences, students can begin to select avenues of personal interest to explore. This allows them to incorporate activities into a lifestyle that promotes movement for life.

Going through this process will help you discover the MOOMBA within you. Remember: "My only obstacle must be attitude." What is keeping your students from fully engaging in your physical education program? What are the obstacles that seem to get in the way of maximizing our potential? By being honest with where we are and where we want to be, we can develop a path with measurable goals. *Maximum Middle School Physical Education* is designed to help you get there.

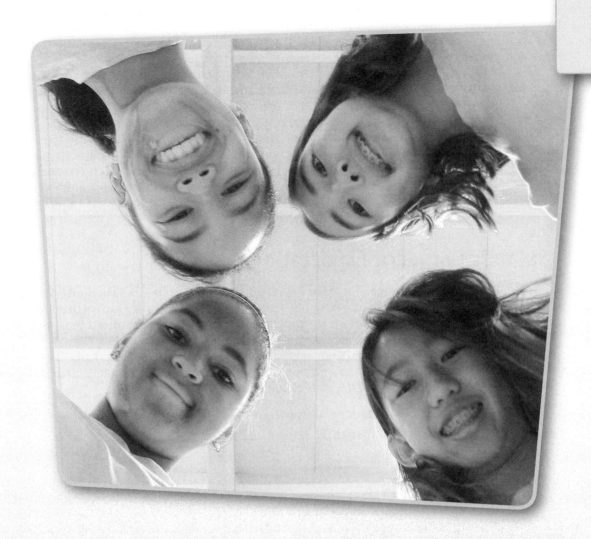

Maximum Learning for All

> **"N**othing can bring you peace but yourself."
>
> —*Ralph Waldo Emerson*

In the introduction to this book, we discussed the four steps to creating a quality program. The next step is to create a learning environment where all students can flourish. How you interact with each child and the subject matter provides a model for students' attitudes toward physical fitness and well-being. You are responsible for creating a positive learning environment by teaching and reinforcing clear expectations for student behavior that is safe, engaging, and respectful.

MOOMBA, which stands for "My only obstacle must be attitude," will help you create that kind of learning space. MOOMBA means more than simply maintaining a positive attitude. It promotes an attitude that has a positive influence on students' choices and how they perceive their experiences, relationships, and the world around them. Through expectations that are clear and consistently enforced, you can foster the type of environment that is necessary for students to develop a positive self-image and respect for others. You have the power to create the reality for students in your classroom, a reality where everyone experiences success and joy in movement. For many students, this is a new reality. The beginning of each school year provides a window of opportunity for building a nurturing classroom environment.

Establish Student Expectations

The priority for any teacher at the beginning of the year is to establish norms for student behavior. Respect, responsibility, perseverance, fairness, courage, trustworthiness, compassion, and citizenship are traits that most educators expect students to demonstrate, yet few take the time to teach students how these traits manifest in action.

It's critical to clearly explain what behaviors you expect from students. Think about the behaviors you want your students to perform in the classroom. Think of the end product and ask yourself these questions:

- What do I want students to know?
- How do I get them there?
- How do I know they got there?

If you want students to be respectful, think about what that behavior would look like and sound like. Once you know what you would like from your students, create learning experiences that teach and reinforce those skills. The students must see the behavior, hear what it sounds like, and practice it. To achieve this, you must consistently

- teach the behaviors you expect;
- reinforce those behaviors through rewards, recognition, and incentives;
- explain why it's important to behave in such a manner; and
- model those behaviors in action.

In addition, placing signs in classrooms, hallways, locker rooms, and so on will provide constant reminders about what is expected

Protect equipment.
Enter and exit quietly.
Attend to directions and follow them the first time.
Cooperate and work well with others.
Expect the best from yourself and from others.

1.1

PQP:
Show What You Know »»»»»

Praise: Name something you liked about the activity.
Question: What did you learn from this experience?
Polish: Describe one way you could make this activity better.

1.2

in student behavior and why. (See reproducibles 1.1 and 1.2, the PEACE and PQP signs, on the CD-ROM.)

Let's consider an example of how a teacher can reinforce positive learning skills when dealing with disruptive students. Rather than becoming reactive to misbehavior and sending students for a time-out (or worse, sending them out of class on a disciplinary referral), the teacher could use the Observation Deck (see page 18) to help students reflect on their behavior and make adjustments so that they can successfully reenter the activity. When students are sent to the Observation Deck, they receive a set of questions to answer before they can return to the activity. They review the skills required for full participation in the activity and understand that the teacher expects everyone to adhere to the behavioral standards.

Assess Yourself

Assessments help us determine if we have reached our goals. If you have purchased an airplane ticket from Los Angeles to Boston, for instance, you will probably determine the success of the airline based on whether you reach Boston on time. If you land in Florida or if the flight is delayed, you will probably think twice about using that airline again.

For an assessment to be valuable, you need to know your destination and when you plan to reach that target goal. A good assessment tool helps you find out what students learned and how well they learned it, and it will often reveal more about the teaching than about student learning. Here lies a fundamental shift in teaching: The teacher assumes responsibility for student learning and uses assessment tools to help improve instruction. When reflecting on student achievement and behavior, student-centered teachers understand that they are responsible for the outcomes in the classroom.

Each lesson should create experiences where students adopt behaviors that foster learning and movement. The purpose of the lesson is reflected in words, behaviors, and interactions. The skills that students learn will benefit them throughout their lives.

Instructional Approaches

Each child is unique and has different strengths in learning. Using multiple teaching strategies increases the likelihood that all students will be exposed to information that they can easily comprehend. Strategies include the following.

- Direct instruction: This is a good technique if you need to give small amounts of information in a short amount of time. It is also a quick and easy way to distribute a large amount of information, but it's difficult to assess whether students understand the material.
- Task teaching: Assign students a task to complete along with a self-assessment tool. Students are provided with examples or a description of how the task should be completed, and then they learn by doing.
- Guided discovery: Provide students with a problem to complete. The results may take different forms, but the students are responsible for resolving the dilemma with the best possible solution.
- Peer teaching: Each student learns a particular skill. Students become experts in their skill and then teach it to their peers.
- Cooperative learning: Students work together to learn a particular skill or complete a task. They share ideas to develop a common understanding of how best to resolve the problem.
- Child-designed instruction: Students create a lesson to present to the class. The lesson they design has the end result of teaching others a new concept or skill.

Environmental Factors

In order to maximize learning, students need an environment where they are motivated to participate and are held accountable for learning, and where learning is reinforced. Being clear and consistent is the key to ensuring that learning will be personalized and become habit. This requires multiple positive learning experiences where students feel safe to take risks. As discussed previously, make sure the expectations for student behaviors are clearly stated, demonstrated, and modeled, and then assess students on what you expect them to learn, holding them accountable for their behavior.

To determine whether you're creating a positive learning environment, it's necessary to reflect on your interactions with students and ask yourself the following questions:

- Do I see what is right in every student or situation and build on it?
- Is the language I use positive?
- Am I joyful when I teach?
- Do I consistently express my positive message in my actions, language, and interactions with all students?

Assess Your Students

As you measure how well students learned what you taught, keep in mind the three domains of learning:

- Cognitive: knowledge about movement, rules, concepts, strategies, and so on
- Affective: feelings, attitudes, relationships, self-esteem, and so on
- Psychomotor: motor skill development (How well can I execute the movement?)

Incorporate assessment tools that indicate mastery in what we know, how we feel, and what we do.

According to the concept of multiple intelligences, every student has different strengths, so it's best to use a variety of tools to assess student performance. Some students have difficulty demonstrating their knowledge verbally and are more apt to show you what they learned through demonstration. Others feel more comfortable writing or drawing what they learned since they have difficulty expressing their thoughts out loud and also don't feel comfortable showing what they learned in front of their peers.

Here are 10 ways students can demonstrate what they have learned (also see table 1.1 on pages 6-7):

1. Student journals: Students keep records of what they have learned or reflect on what they experienced. This can help students identify attitudes about movement or social interactions that enhance or impede participation or performance.
2. Exit slips: Quick way for students to share important concepts or facts with the teacher before leaving class.
3. Homework: Provides an incentive for continued practice at home or over the weekend.
4. Peer observations: Students observe other students performing a task and developing a skill to make suggestions for improvement or to learn how to improve themselves.
5. Skill demonstrations: Students must perform a specific skill or event, such as making 3 out of 5 baskets or performing a forward pass.
6. Videotaping: Students view themselves performing a skill and assess their own performance against a rubric.

7. Student drawings: Students draw a diagram of a concept or skill.

8. Student displays: Students present a display that illustrates what they have learned.

9. Teacher observations: Teacher assesses students' learning by monitoring daily performance.

10. Portfolios: Students collect artifacts that reflect growth over a period of time, such as performance charts, graphs, pictures, and so on.

Maximize Learning Time

Time is a valuable resource, and each minute is an opportunity to maximize student learning. Is the lesson structured to make the most of the time you have with your students? A good goal is to have students actively engaged in learning for at least 70 percent of the class. Figure 1.1 shows the structure of a typical 55-minute class.

Students must have the confidence to take risks and be supportive of others' learning. They must practice positive social skills and learn how to speak and act in ways that support a positive learning environment for all students. Maximize on-task activity by asking yourself the following questions.

Sample Lesson Structure

Roll call	2 minutes
Dress	5 minutes
Instruction	5 minutes
Equipment checkout	1 minute
Activity time	27 minutes
Debriefing	3 minutes
Equipment check-in	2 minutes
Dress	10 minutes

FIGURE 1.1 Structure of a typical 55-minute class.

- Are there different challenges for students with different abilities? Set out equipment that meets students at their skill level. Include different ball sizes, obstacle lengths or heights, or movement complexities. This allows students to choose a challenge they can be successful at or to stretch their skills.

- Is there enough equipment so that every student can practice the skill without waiting in line? When lines are necessary, take a moment to time how long students must wait for a turn to participate. They should wait no longer than 40 seconds.

- Is there success for all at a level that is appropriate for each student? It's crucial to consider the needs of all students, including students with disabilities. For example, if students are shooting a basketball through the hoop, do you provide modifications so everyone experiences success? This question focuses not on allowing students to choose the degree of difficulty but on structuring the activity so as to allow for maximum success.

Explain and Enforce Department Procedures

Middle school students are interesting creatures. Their job is to find every loophole, every ambiguity, and the exception to every rule. You can make your job much easier by using the first few weeks of school to concentrate on class procedures. Communicating clearly to students where to report, how to enter the locker room, what to wear, where to dress, how to exit the locker room, and how to act when waiting for roll call will greatly benefit your class throughout the rest of the year. In addition to students seeing and practicing these behaviors, you should reinforce them often.

Table 1.1 Types of Assessment

Sample assessment	Description	Psychomotor: What you do	Cognitive: What you know	Affective: How you feel
Student journals	Students keep records of their performance and attitudes over time. Usually each entry is a response to a teacher prompt or a reflection on goals.	Students keep a running record of time, distance, or reps completed. Example: Students record their mile time on a graph for four months.	Students respond to a prompt that allows them to reflect on the execution of a skill or response to a time. Students develop a plan to improve performance and measure outcomes. Example: Students develop a strategy to improve their mile time and record their progress.	Students describe how they are feeling or how their body is feeling in response to a task. Students reflect on how they can improve performance through effort, teamwork, or attitude. Example: Students share how they felt with each run and compare their feelings to their exercise and recovery heart rates.
Exit slips	Students must have an appropriate response to exit the class or an activity. The teacher is looking for a specific response. Response can be oral, written, or a physical response.	Students perform a skill using the correct technique. Example: Students show correct technique used in a push-up.	Students describe proper execution on a particular skill or share an important concept related to physical education. Example: Students share a fitness activity and what component of fitness it addresses.	Students respond to a prompt that describes how they can improve performance through effort, teamwork, or attitude. Example: Students assess how they perceived their performance in a task and how to improve it.
Homework	Students continue practice of a skill or create an artifact that demonstrates understanding beyond the class time.	Students are provided an assessment sheet for a parent or guardian to sign to verify they completed a task. Example: Students must complete five rotations of a juggling cascade for parent signature, or students diagram a basic cascade.	Students are able to correctly complete the assigned task and communicate with others the important components of the task or concept. Example: Students can share the skills required to complete a basic cascade.	Students are able to share their homework assignment with others and communicate pride in their completed work. Example: Students share the effort required to complete the task and are eager to demonstrate a basic cascade.
Peer observations	Students observe other students perform a task or skill and learn from their performance, or coach the other student.	Students perform a task and perfect the skill through student feedback or by learning from another student's performance. Example: Students observe another student perform a volley tennis serve and are able to make suggestions to improve based on a rubric or skill chart.	Students are able to communicate to one another the skills required for execution of a task. They are able to assess and coach one another. Example: Students are able to provide feedback and explain why it is important.	Students are positive and encouraging to others and are able to receive feedback. Example: Students are providing constructive feedback in a positive manner. Feedback is well received.
Skill demonstrations	Students are able to demonstrate a task using proper form and technique.	Students execute the task correctly. Example: Students are able to perform a slap shot correctly.	Students are able to describe how to execute a task correctly and provide the reasons why it is important to use proper technique. Example: Students are able to share why correct technique is important in the slap shot.	Students exert effort and are persistent in executing a task correctly. Example: Students are exerting effort and persistence in mastering the slap shot. If not, they are able to communicate why.

Sample assessment	Description	Psychomotor: What you do	Cognitive: What you know	Affective: How you feel
Videotaping	Student performance is recorded and viewed by students.	Students are able to improve performance through visual feedback. Example: Students view themselves performing a football pass and are able to correct their performance.	Students are able to describe what they are doing well and what they need to improve. Example: Students are able to share what is incorrect in their performance and explain what they need to do to improve and why it is important.	Students are insightful and eager to improve performance. Example: Students are eager to view their tape and improve on their performance, as demonstrated through thoughtful comments about how they will improve their performance.
Student drawings	Students draw a response to a prompt.	Students are able to diagram movement patterns or important elements required for a task. Example: Students draw an offensive pattern in basketball.	Students are able to communicate why movement patterns are selected and strengths and weaknesses of the patterns. Example: Students draw an offensive pattern and are able to provide information about how it is best used.	Students are able to share how they feel about a task and areas of strength or areas of improvement. Example: Students are able to draw an offensive pattern in basketball and share what they feel is required to best execute the plan.
Student displays	Students report or demonstrate movement skills, concepts, or strategies.	Students are able to execute movement patterns that demonstrate mastery of a concept or skill. Example: Students create a display board that highlights important concepts in physical fitness.	Students are able to describe important concepts and skills. Example: Students are able to communicate in the fitness display board what muscle groups benefit from a particular exercise.	Students are able to share elements of group dynamics or personal growth strategies. Example: Students are able to share what attitudes are required to be successful in becoming fit.
Teacher observations	Teacher observes students at work and makes assessments based on their performance.	Teacher observes students executing a task correctly. Example: Teacher observes students using positive comments for social skill development: "Nice try, Bill."	Teacher is able to assess that students understand the principles of movement through their ability to adjust to changing situations. Example: Teacher observes students being specific with their positive comments to encourage and improve a classmate's performance: "Way to use your legs, Bill."	Teacher observes students' interactions with others and is able to determine effort and attitude through verbal or visual cues. Example: Teacher observes students observing others and being conscientious about making positive comments: "Bill, I really liked the way we worked together to achieve our goal."
Portfolios	Students collect several artifacts from a variety of resources to demonstrate mastery of a skill or concept.	Students communicate through pictures or writing correct psychomotor skills. Example: Students submit a juggling report that includes key concepts in juggling, a checklist of their last performance, and a feedback form on how to improve.	Students are able to communicate key concepts that lead to proper execution of a skill. Example: Students are able to communicate the strategies used to teach juggling.	Students communicate what they have learned and how they feel about their learning. Example: Students are able to communicate what got in the way of performance and what helped their performance. Students are able to provide a strategy on how to improve performance.

Clothing

Explain what you expect students to wear during class (e.g., shoes, socks, shirt, shorts, or sweats). If school physical education uniforms are available for purchase, inform students how much they cost, as well as when and where they can be purchased. Have a student wear the uniform and show examples of what not to wear. Be sure to explain why it's important to dress properly—students are more apt to comply when they know why.

In addition, inform students when you expect them to dress. Add a notice in the summer mailer so parents know where they can purchase a uniform or what students are expected to wear on the first dress day. Explain the benefits of physical activity and why it's important for their children to dress appropriately. Communicate with the counseling staff or outreach personnel to determine which students may need assistance to acquire a uniform, and work with your school to provide the uniform so that all students can fully participate in the activities.

Roll Call

Provide students with assigned seats for roll call. A good strategy is to assign numbers to student names. You can easily copy the attendance roster where student names are listed by number. Each student's number on the roster becomes his or her magic number, or the place where he or she sits for class. The numbers are painted on the floor or on benches; alternately, poly spots can be purchased that have numbers on them, but two disadvantages are that they can be heavy and they must be set up every day. Magic numbers can add excitement and intrigue to the mundane task of roll call. (For details on using magic numbers, see page 9.)

Students are expected to be on their numbers on time. Clearly explain to students what that looks like; for example, students are expected to be sitting on their magic numbers 5 minutes after the tardy bell. Don't forget to practice reporting to roll call—excuse students to the locker rooms and then have them immediately report to their numbers until they can complete the task in an acceptable amount of time. Have fun with it!

While seated on their numbers, students are expected to be quiet, facing front, dressed, and using active listening (e.g., seated, hands on lap, eyes facing forward, shoulders square to the teacher, and mouths closed). Spend time during the first couple of weeks working on this skill with all students. Repeat the exercise if students are not all seated, facing the front, and using active listening. It's vital to reinforce this standard of behavior and revisit it throughout the year when required.

Gym Behavior

The gym is where learning takes place. Give explicit guidelines for how you expect students to enter the gym and then have them practice that behavior. If you frequent other facilities, such as a cafeteria, multipurpose room, or pool, have students practice the protocol for entering those facilities as well. For example, students should enter the facility single file without talking and sit in an assigned area while waiting for instructions.

Teacher preparation is critical to the success of on-task behavior. You should be aware of the discipline required to complete such a task and be prepared to engage students promptly when everyone is ready to learn. Before the students enter the facility, have any equipment, stations, and cues ready.

Where to Meet

Indicate where you would like students to meet for the remainder of the week. The first week of school is highly stressful for students, so post signs throughout campus to ensure that everyone knows where to meet. Make sure office staff are also aware so they can easily direct students to the correct location.

Establish Class Management Protocols

Once students have practiced how to begin class in various locations, you can dedicate a space to begin each day. Students will know where to report each day unless directed differently on a bulletin board. A bulletin board that is centrally located to provide information that students need to know will allow you to maximize the time for movement activities. Students will be seated and ready for instructions and movement in any of the facilities used, because they will have practiced where to go and how to assemble there.

Magic Numbers

Magic numbers are roll-call numbers that tell students where to sit while waiting for instructions and for attendance. You can use these numbers in a variety of ways to add excitement. For example, assign an animal such as a bear, wolf, eagle, and so on to each set of numbers. (Most middle school students are intrigued by animals.) To strengthen character development and highlight traits you would like students to have, you can also assign traits associated with that animal, such as courage for the lion, cooperation for the wolf, vision for the eagle, and so on. The name of the animal or trait is stenciled at the base of the set. When students read the sign, they will see that they are assigned to report to the eagle station, for example. This designation makes it easier for students to recognize where they are to meet each day or for specific activities. As students become more accustomed to the area, they will know where the eagle station is located and report without hesitation or required direction.

In addition, you can use magic numbers for a variety of fun activities. The two activities that follow are examples of how magic numbers not only can aid in taking roll quickly but also can provide a home base for students and help create a positive tone to your class.

The Lottery

The Lottery is a creative, fair, and fun way to select student helpers. You will need roll-call numbers painted, written in chalk, or placed on poly spots to complete this activity.

Select a number from those available. Inform the students that after completing a warm-up run, they must select a number upon their return. When students return, they can stand on any number they choose—first come, first served. Only one student is allowed on each number. One of those numbers (or more if needed) is the lottery number. Once all students have returned and are standing on a number, announce the number or numbers you've chosen. The students on the lottery numbers will be the teacher's assistants for the day or part of the How Can I Help You Crew (see page 10). If the lottery number is vacant when everyone returns, meaning no one is standing on the lottery number, announce, "No one has selected the lottery number." Students are then allowed to change numbers. This works best when there is more than one lottery number up for grabs.

Random Acts of Kindness

This is a variation on the Lottery. Prepare a bag that contains all of the numbers from roll call. Each student has an assigned magic number (the daily roll-call magic number). Select a number from the bag and give that student two positive comments and a goodie (such as a certificate, sticker, and so on). The selected student then picks another number from the bag. That student gives two positive comments to the student whose number was drawn, and the teacher provides a goodie for the first student to present to the second. Then the second student takes another number from the bag, and the random acts of kindness continue.

This activity is most effective when done during 5 minutes at the beginning of class. Initially, many students will feel uncomfortable giving as well as receiving compliments. It's important that the behavior is modeled and that students practice giving positive comments. Through repetition, you can create an environment that is accepting and affirming.

Reinforcing Positive Behaviors With Peers

The following activities provide structured learning experiences that help students develop peer-to-peer communication that is appropriate, safe, and nurturing. Students must hear what you expect them to say, so be very specific on what you expect as they greet, praise, and provide feedback to one another.

Three Hs

In this activity, students learn how to respectfully greet an adult. When exiting at the end of the class, each student can choose whether to say good-bye to you with a handshake, with a high five, or by saying hello. You don't initiate the greeting but respond to each student's choice. The activity develops the students' ability to interact positively with others, and this must be encouraged and modeled by you.

Put-Ups

It is your responsibility to ensure that students do not use put-downs when others are trying to perform new tasks. This activity helps develop a culture where students encourage each other and help each other take risks by giving put-ups. Group initiatives are instrumental in helping students develop the language of put-ups.

Have the class think about put-ups they can use to encourage others. They will usually come up with "nice try," "nice hit," or "good work." Help them learn to be more specific with their words, and give points to students who use them during class. Take time at the end of class to point out positive put-ups you heard and recognize the students who used them.

Healthy Helpfuls

Place inspirational comments on the information board (see page 11) for students' reflection. For example, students are asked to say a put-up to a teacher, to hug a parent when they get home, or to take a pet for a walk. Create a positive environment, and remind students that these behaviors continue beyond the classroom. Take time to review the comments on the board and why they are important to you. Why do we value honesty, responsibility, and caring behaviors, and how do they make others feel?

How Can I Help You Crew

Students must learn how to care for equipment and assist in maintaining a positive learning environment. The How Can I Help You Crew consists of students who assist you with equipment setup, takedown, inventory, and storage. You may select students to serve on the crew, but all students have the opportunity to volunteer and seek ways to help you—for example, by setting up equipment before roll call or staying after to help clean up. Your expectations of the crew must be made public so all students understand that they are part of the How Can I Help You Crew.

28	21	14	7
27	20	13	6
26	19	12	5
25	18	11	4
24	17	10	3
23	16	9	2
22*	15*	8*	1*

FIGURE 1.2 In this arrangement of 28 children, students 1 through 7 are in one pod, with student 1 as pod leader. *Pod leader.

Pods

Dolphins swim in pods, a place of safety where everyone depends on each other to survive. Assign students to pods within their class. Each pod has a pod leader responsible for collecting equipment, making sure instructions are appropriately carried out, and representing the group (see figure 1.2).

You could just as easily assign students to prides or herds instead of pods. The point is to be consistent with a theme that reinforces the behavior you would like students to demonstrate each day.

Information Board

Write your name boldly on a sign and indicate where you expect students to meet you for roll call. Post this sign on the information board, as well as daily agendas or directions for class. Train students to read the board before sitting in roll-call order. Have pod leaders read the board and then inform their group members or have a field reporter for the day announce the agenda and activity (see page 17).

Before-Class Challenges

Before-class challenges are tasks that take place before class time. Students get in their pods and work as a team to complete challenges that may be mental or physical. Students earn points for their team as they work together to complete the tasks.

Figure 1.3 is an example of a before-class challenge, and figure 1.4 is an example of a picture puzzle. On the CD-ROM, you will find 17 before-class challenges and 17 picture puzzles. (See reproducibles 1.3 and 1.4, the PE Challenges and PE Puzzles, on the CD-ROM.) Here are the solutions to all the picture puzzles:

1. Hole in one
2. Basketball
3. Defense
4. Badminton
5. Boxing
6. High jump
7. Spike
8. Two points
9. Backward jump rope
10. Quarter
11. Archery
12. Racquetball
13. Gymnastics
14. Captain
15. Hockey
16. Tee ball
17. Jumping jacks

Get Off to a Good Start

The first 2 to 3 weeks of school are critical in teaching and training students in class expectations and protocols. How you approach this orientation will determine how successful students will be throughout the year. The length of time you spend on orientation activities depends on many variables. However, the outcome of what you expect in student behavior must be clear to you and communicated in behavioral terms to the students. What do you expect them to do? If you want students to listen when you speak, for example, you must train students to face you with their shoulders square, eyes on you, hands in the lap, and mouths closed.

Following are activities I have found helpful in establishing a positive learning environment.

Weeks 1 and 2

As discussed earlier, the first weeks of school provide a window of opportunity to establish class protocols. Following is a schedule of events that promote a positive learning environment. Because physical education classes are usually in the open and seen by other teachers, it helps to have every teacher within the department agree on class procedures and promote the same procedures for every student. This helps prevent students from saying something such as, "But that teacher lets his students wear pants under their shorts, so why don't you?"

PE Challenge 1

Beanbag Toss

Each team member attempts to toss beanbags into the bucket. All players must stay outside the circle.

- 3 points for inside the bucket
- 2 points for inside the inner circle

Do not retrieve any beanbags until *every* beanbag has been tossed.

How many points did your team make?

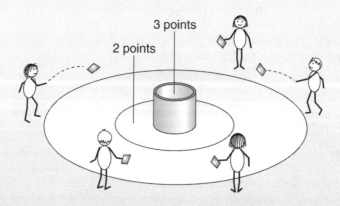

1.3a

FIGURE 1.3 Sample before-class challenge.

PE Puzzle 1

1

Answer

_____

1.4a

FIGURE 1.4 Sample picture puzzle.

Use the first week for students to get to know you and their classmates, as well as learn about department policies, class procedures, and the curriculum.

Day 1: Icebreakers

When students feel that you know them, they are more apt to cooperate with you and each other. Getting to know your students through icebreaker activities helps create a strong foundation for teaching respect and responsibility for each other's learning. Many schools designate specific days for these types of activities, so coordinate with teachers in other departments to complement each other's work.

Following are four icebreakers that can be used during the first day of class. Student Bingo and Yellow Brick Road Scavenger Hunt get students moving and interacting right away. The T-shirt and totem pole activities require some individual reflection before sharing, which allows time for the first-day logistics to take place (e.g., locker distribution, picture day, and so on) while students work on their project.

Student Bingo

Each student receives a bingo card and writes the name of a classmate who meets each criteria on the bingo squares. Students who fill up the card have scored a bingo. (See reproducible 1.5, "Student Bingo," on the CD-ROM.)

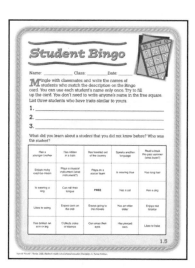

Yellow Brick Road Scavenger Hunt

In this variation on Student Bingo, students receive a sheet that has different quests. They must find someone who has slept in a tent, someone who likes to swim, and so on. They mingle within the class, writing the name of a student who has completed each task. (See reproducible 1.6, "Yellow Brick Road Scavenger Hunt," on the CD-ROM.)

Design Your Own Logo

Students receive an outline of a T-shirt on a piece of paper and design a logo that best captures their interests. Students are placed in groups of four and share their designs with each other. If time permits, students get into different groups and share their designs again. (See reproducible 1.7, "Design Your Own Logo," on the CD-ROM.)

Design Your Own Totem Pole

Students receive a piece of paper with the outline of a totem pole. They design segments of their pole to illustrate significant accomplishments, events, or people in their lives. Students are placed in groups of four and share their totem pole with each other. (See reproducible 1.8, "Design Your Own Totem Pole," on the CD-ROM.)

Day 2: Class Expectations

When communicating your expectations, you must state them simply but in a positive manner to encourage positive behavior. A good example would be, "We come to class prepared to learn and are respectful of the learning environment." This is a simple rule that all students should be able to repeat and reflect on as they participate throughout the class. If students come to class without proper attire, they can reflect on the class expectations and know that they have not lived up to the commitment to learn. If they make fun of another student, they are reminded of the class expectations and know they have violated the learning environment.

Set the Tone

Introduce rules to set the tone in your class by encouraging students to behave in an appropriate manner. Clear expectations result in appropriate behavior. To reinforce the tone, hang posters throughout the classroom and building to establish what you expect from students, and offer school activities, recognition programs, and so on that focus on character development. Following are examples of class-, department-, or schoolwide themes that provide clear expectations for student behavior.

- Positive and student driven: Students will come prepared to learn and be respectful of the learning environment.
- Three Rs: Respect, responsibility, relationships. Students will be respectful, be responsible, and value their relationships with others.
- PPP: Students will be positive, productive, and polite.
- PEP: Students will be positive, encouraging, and patient.

Establish Management Protocols

Practice transitions with the students. Explain how you expect them to move from place to place by preparing an area where they should report to. While they are sitting on their numbers, explain the value of working together as a team within their pod, how leaders will be assigned, and the leaders' responsibilities.

Designate a pod leader for this exercise. Point to the farthest row to your right and the farthest row to your left. The rows in between must align themselves between the two points. Before the rows leave for their new location, ask the pod leaders to look to their left and right so they can align themselves in the same formation. The challenge is to see how quickly the entire class can form their pods in the same roll-call formation in the new spot. Since you are requesting students to be respectful and responsible, it's important that you stress cooperation, not competition.

Go to the new spot and see how quickly the class can establish themselves in row formation. You can time them, encouraging students to help each other. The time stops when the class is seated, facing the front, with their hands on their laps and their mouths closed. This should be practiced often, but initially it should be done in a fun, enthusiastic manner.

Show an Orientation Video

An orientation video is a great way for students to learn by seeing and hearing your expectations for the class. Enlisting more experienced students to star in the video adds great interest and takes only a day of filming. The benefits of creating an orientation video are well worth the investment. The CD-ROM contains a sample script to use when making a video. (See reproducible 1.9, "Sample Script for Orientation Video," on the CD-ROM.)

Sample Script for Orientation Video

Students must be able to see and hear what is expected of them. Following is a script for an orientation video that you can adapt to meet your needs. Ask for volunteers to be actors in your video, and play the video during the first week of each school year. You will be surprised how student performance improves when you provide clear expectations for behavior.

Scene 1

Teacher in the gym with students playing in the background

Teacher: Welcome to physical education, where you will learn some fun skills and have a great time, too. But there are some important things you need to know to be successful throughout the year.

Scene 2

Students in the locker room

Student 1: This is where every class begins in the locker room. Each student will receive a locker to store PE clothes in and to store school clothes in during class. A locker is kind of like having your own closet, only much smaller. Remember, never give your locker combination to anyone, including friends.

Student 2: Please make sure your locker is locked before you leave for class and at the end of each day. Oh, and another note about lockers. Don't bring anything of value to school and never leave anything of value in your PE locker. Always keep valuables with you or give them to your teacher or locker-room attendant. I'm sure you will be tempted to bring that really cool CD or video game to school, but trust me, there will be people out there who would love to have it, too. So, take my advice and leave those things at home, where you know they will be safe.

(continued)

1.9

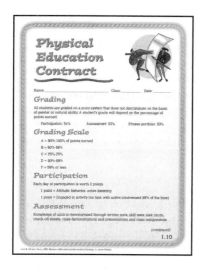

Introduce a Contract

Whatever expectations you establish for your class, make them simple and easy to remember. A contract for students to sign that clearly states the rules will leave no question that student behavior is a high priority. The key to success is to state all expectations in positive terms, make sure students understand why the standards exist, and generate student support for the class expectations. Students will feel they are on a learning adventure and experience the joy of traveling with you. (See reproducible 1.10, "Physical Education Contract," on the CD-ROM.)

Lead Class-Climate Activities

Construct a positive class climate by including activities that help students practice the skills you expect from them as they interact throughout the year. Teaching appropriate interactions requires supervised activities where the speech and actions are modeled and practiced. Activities that could be used include the following:

- Three Hs (page 10)
- Hi, How Are You? Gotta Go (page 35)
- Random Acts of Kindness (page 9)

Day 3: Practicing Class Procedures and Expectations

Day 3 allows students to practice what they have learned. Take a moment before class to train student helpers to assist others. Place roll-call numbers on the information board and greet students as they enter, reminding them of your expectation that they sit on their numbers, facing the front.

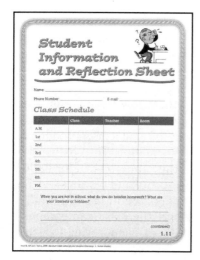

- Review the instructions for opening the lockers and where to get help if needed.
- Hand out locker assignments and have students copy their locker combinations in their notebooks.
- Send students to the locker room to practice opening their locker.
- Remind students to keep their combinations private and secure their locks when they are finished dressing.
- Provide students with personal reflection sheets to keep them occupied while they wait for their locker assignments or if they finish early. (See reproducible 1.11, "Student Information and Reflection Sheet," on the CD-ROM.)

Weeks 2 and 3

Use the second and third weeks of school to teach specific skills you expect from students throughout the year. The following team initiatives (pages 18-39) develop class management techniques, social skills, and teamwork. Have fun and make sure to debrief each activity and clearly state to students what you expect of them during class time.

Seven Great Guidelines for Creating a MOOMBA Environment

MOOMBA involves creating an environment of success for every child. As a teacher, you establish the ground rules for how students will interact with each other and the subject matter. Your expectations should be high, positively communicated, modeled, and reinforced with each interaction between teacher and students as well as between students themselves. Remember that every activity you introduce should serve a common purpose: improving student achievement. To maximize learning, the stage should be set for each segment of instruction.

> The teacher knows and applies effective teaching strategies that provide maximum student time on task . . . the instructional program is planned to provide for involvement, and for optimal achievement, by all students. (NASPE, 1998)

1. Develop Adherence to Teacher Directives

Create situations to help students develop their listening skills and ability to follow directions. Students must be able to immediately follow your directives on one command.

2. Stay on Task

Have confidence that students will do the right thing, even with little or no direction from you. This requires that you make sure the physical environment is engaging and free from attractive nuisances (i.e., items students can throw, swing on, or climb) and areas students can roam into (i.e., bathrooms, locker rooms, equipment rooms, blind spots on the field).

3. Use an Information Board

Create one place where students can find out what is scheduled for the day. Include information you expect students to know before the lesson that day (see page 11).

4. Assign Field Reporters

Select a field reporter or assign the pod leaders to inform the class what is happening for the day. The field reporter reads the bulletin on the way to the roll-call assembly area. Make this activity fun by pretending to be a news anchor seeking the news from the field reporter. Find an old microphone, hat, or badge that the field reporter can use.

5. Practice Moving From Place to Place

During the first 2 weeks of school, the class should practice moving from place to place. Take the time to train students how to move from station to station. Students must know what you expect of them when time is up at their station, such as putting equipment back where they found it or getting down on one knee and looking at you ("Down on one knee and look at me") when the music stops. They must also know how to examine the equipment when they arrive at a station, as well as how to care for the equipment, use it properly, and look for any damage.

6. Catch Them Doing It Right

Take every opportunity to use students' names in identifying what they are doing right. Be specific and describe what the student is doing. This will allow other students to learn your expectations for behavior. For example, you might say, "Way to go, Kevin, you're using encouraging words by telling Sharon that she can do it," or, "Nice job, Mary, you're seated and using your listening skills, facing forward, and your eyes are on me."

7. Use a Whistle System

Create a whistle system to make sure students comply with an immediate request to sit and remain still. The whistle indicates that you need to provide more information for the lesson, or that there is an emergency and you need to attend to it. An example could be three long, loud whistles, which signal students to get down on one knee and look for you. This system must be practiced throughout the year to ensure a safe environment is maintained in case of an emergency.

Observation Deck

OBJECTIVE

Classroom management

EQUIPMENT

Hula hoop, cones, bench, or tarp; 2 or 3 laminated cards

SETUP

Create laminated cards with three questions:
- What will I **stop** doing?
- What will I **start** doing?
- What will I **continue** doing?

Create the observation deck using a hula hoop, cones, a bench, or a tarp.

DIRECTIONS

1. Tell students that if they act inappropriately, they will go to the observation deck to observe appropriate classroom behavior for 15 to 30 seconds, reflecting on their behavior and making a choice to change it.
2. When students act inappropriately, give them a card and send them to the observation deck to reflect on the three questions.
3. Students determine when they are ready to leave the observation deck but must spend at least 15 to 30 seconds there.
4. They return the card to you and share their response to the three questions when they are ready to participate in an appropriate manner.
5. Debrief the student to review appropriate behavior after class, if necessary.

> ⚠ SAFETY TIP
>
> The observation deck must be in full view and close enough to you that students can hear your instructions.

TEACHING TIPS

- Immediately upon the student returning the card or after the lesson, listen to the student's response to the three questions.
- Successful use of the observation deck requires that students know its purpose: to observe other students performing appropriate behavior and reflect on their own behavior.
- Make sure students reenter the activity with a readiness to make appropriate choices. They need to understand that they are responsible for regulating their behavior.
- If students continue to misbehave, you may require them to remain in the observation deck for the remainder of the activity and then have a student–teacher conference immediately following the activity. If the pattern continues, you may be required to follow the school discipline policy, call the student's home, or place the student on restricted activity until ready to fully participate with the class.

VARIATION

Students can memorize the three questions if cards are not available. They must make contact with you, such as giving you a high five, before answering the questions to reenter the activity.

Mingle

OBJECTIVE

Classroom management

EQUIPMENT

Whistle

SETUP

This activity requires a well-defined space. Before conducting the activity, demonstrate how to mingle by walking through a group, making eye contact with other students, smiling, and greeting others as they pass.

DIRECTIONS

1. Students spread out within the playing area.
2. Blow the whistle and inform students how to group themselves, such as the following:
   - Get into groups of three.
   - Get into groups of five.
   - Get into groups with students who have the same birth month.
   - Get into groups that have the same color of socks.
   - Get into groups that eat the same cereal.
3. Once students are in groups, tell students to mingle.
4. Repeat steps 2 and 3 as desired.

TEACHING TIPS

- The goal of this activity is to train students to listen to your directions when you blow the whistle. It's a fun activity that has huge benefits for classroom management throughout the entire school year.
- When you ask students to get into groups, they learn to do it quickly and not spend time trying to get into groups with their friends, leaving other students feeling ostracized.

VARIATION

Whistle Mixer: Students move throughout the area. When you blow the whistle, they must get into groups that match the number of times the whistle was blown, such as the following:

- If you blow the whistle three times, students must form groups of three.
- If you blow the whistle five times, students must form groups of five.

This forces students to listen and follow directions.

Fruits of Your Labor

OBJECTIVE

Classroom management

EQUIPMENT

None

SETUP

This activity requires a well-defined space. Before beginning, demonstrate each command and show students how to move within the space.

DIRECTIONS

1. Students spread out in the playing area.
2. Call out the name of a fruit, to which students must respond quickly but in a safe manner.
   - Grapes: Students gather around you, getting down on one knee within your view.
   - Apples: Students stand where they are.
   - Bananas: Students disperse within the playing area.
   - Oranges: Students sit where they are.
   - Fruit punch: Students lie down quietly where they are and relax.
3. When all students are performing the task correctly and are quiet, call out another formation.
4. Repeat until all students are performing all formations correctly.

> ### ⚠ SAFETY TIP
>
> The importance of this exercise cannot be overemphasized. Not only will it make transitions easier, but it may also become necessary in the event of an emergency, when you need students to stop their activity and immediately lie down or report to you.
>
> Running is not allowed. Students can move quickly but feet must be in contact with the floor at all times by using the heel–toe technique (students keep contact with the floor by ensuring the heel of the lead leg touches the floor before they lift the toes of the back foot off the floor). Teach the heel–toe technique and ensure students respond to that cue.

TEACHING TIPS

- In this activity, students learn to move quickly from space to space and change formations to receive instructions or begin an activity. Spend as much time as necessary to ensure all students are performing the tasks correctly, especially grapes. The students must be silent and performing the task correctly before you call out another command.

- Praise students for performing the tasks correctly.
- Revisit this exercise throughout the year so that it becomes automatic. In case of an emergency, you know students will comply quickly and quietly.

VARIATION

You can create any set of names to identify different formations. The important concept is for students to immediately comply with the command.

Rock, Paper, Scissors

OBJECTIVE

Getting to know other students

EQUIPMENT

None

SETUP

This activity requires a well-defined space. Before beginning, demonstrate how to play Rock, Paper, Scissors with another student.

DIRECTIONS

1. Ask students to get into groups of two and play Rock, Paper, Scissors. No score is kept.
2. Students face each other with their left palm up. They use their right arm and hand as a hammer, striking their right fist three times on their left palm. On the third strike, they reveal one of the following options:
   - Rock—A fist remains on their left palm. Rock breaks scissors.
   - Paper—The right hand is placed palm down on their left palm. Paper covers rock.
   - Scissors—The right index and middle finger are extended in a V, indicating scissors. Scissors cut paper.
3. Students play three rounds and then find new partners and start again.

TEACHING TIPS

- This activity allows students to meet and interact with everyone in the class quickly, easily, and without competition or stress. The pace should move quickly, with students searching to find others to play with.
- Use Rock, Paper, Scissors to resolve disagreements. For example, if a ball was called out but another student disagreed, the students could use Rock, Paper, Scissors to determine the outcome and quickly move on with the activity.

VARIATION

Students get into groups of two and play Rock, Paper, Scissors as explained above. In each pair, the winner moves over to a designated Success Zone, and the loser moves over to a designated Try Again Zone. Students in each zone pair up and play another round of Rock, Paper, Scissors, again moving to the Success Zone or the Try Again Zone based on the results. Students keep playing rounds with new partners, running back and forth between the zones as needed. (If a student who is already in the Success Zone wins the round, he or she remains in that zone. Similarly, if a student already in the Try Again Zone loses the round, he or she remains in that zone.)

Finger Trap

OBJECTIVE

Getting to know other students

EQUIPMENT

None

SETUP

Have students form a circle, standing elbow to elbow, and then drop their hands to their sides.

DIRECTIONS

1. Students stand in a circle with their hands stretched out from their sides. Their right hands are palm up under their right partner's left hand, which is facing down. Their left hands are palm down over their left partner's right hand, which is facing up.
2. Say, "Ready position." Students place their pointed left index finger on the right palm of the student to their left.
3. Say, "Go!" Students try to grab the index finger on their right while simultaneously trying to escape the grasp of the student on their left.
4. Repeat several times.

> ⚠ SAFETY TIP
>
> Demonstrate appropriate snatching techniques. Stress the need to be respectful and use appropriate touch.

TEACHING TIP

This activity provides a place for students to touch each other in an appropriate manner. It establishes that appropriate physical contact with other students is a natural and common occurrence in movement activities.

Pulse

OBJECTIVES

Cooperation, teamwork

EQUIPMENT

None

SETUP

None

DIRECTIONS

1. Students form a circle by holding hands with the person on their right and left. You join the circle as well.
2. Start the pulse by squeezing the hand of the student to your left or right.
3. The student sends the pulse to the next person.
4. Continue until the pulse has traveled around the circle back to you.

> ⚠ **SAFETY TIP**
>
> You must demonstrate an appropriate versus an inappropriate hand squeeze.

TEACHING TIP

Students must be taught how to send a pulse that is respectful. Be sure to explain exactly what you expect of them.

VARIATIONS

- Have the originator send multiple squeezes or send squeezes in both directions.
- See if the group can complete the task without talking.
- Time how long a pulse takes to go around the circle or create record times for the students to beat.

Hula-Hula

OBJECTIVES

Cooperation, teamwork

EQUIPMENT

1 hula hoop for every 12 students

SETUP

This exercise is similar to the Pulse, except that the students must send a hula hoop around the circle while holding hands. For maximum participation, place several hula hoops throughout the circle, but make sure students send the hoops in the same direction.

DIRECTIONS

1. Students form a circle, holding hands.
2. Place several hula hoops around the wrists of two students. The number of hula hoops will vary depending on the size of the class. A good rule of thumb is to have a 1:12 ratio. For instance, if there are 50 students in a class, have four hula hoops ready for the activity.
3. Instruct students not to release their grasp on the student to their left or right.
4. Through their body movements, students must move the hula hoop clockwise around the circle until it returns to the original position.

TEACHING TIPS

- This activity is fun and difficult, but it can be done. Students need to communicate and be supportive of one another.
- After the task, ask students what they learned from the activity. Ask them how they can complete the task more quickly.
- Use different-colored hula hoops and bandannas. This allows for easy identification when a hula hoop has successfully reached its destination.

VARIATIONS

- For an extra challenge, have students send two hoops in opposite directions starting at opposite points in the circle.
- Bandanna's Comet: Students form a circle with both hands holding a tied climbing rope. Students send four bandannas that are tied to the rope around the circle until they reach their starting point. Designate one student as a home base for each bandanna. Use the same debrief questions as for Hula-Hula.

Partner Get-Up

OBJECTIVES

Cooperation, teamwork

EQUIPMENT

None

SETUP

Space approximately the size of a basketball court

DIRECTIONS

1. Ask students to mingle.

2. Direct them to find a student who is a similar size, stand back to back, and interlock their arms.

3. Ask students to sit on the floor while remaining interlocked with their partner.

4. Now ask them to stand without losing contact. They must apply their force equally to support their sit and get-up positions.

5. Repeat with new partners.

TEACHING TIPS

- Students are becoming more intimate with body proximity. Encourage students to communicate and problem solve to be successful.
- Move quickly so students do not have an opportunity to be selective when choosing partners.

VARIATION

Try groups of 3 or 4 students.

Group Get-Up

OBJECTIVES

Cooperation, teamwork, communication

EQUIPMENT

75-foot (23-meter) climbing rope, with ends tied in a no-slip knot to form a circle

SETUP

The rope should be placed in the center of the circle the students will form.

DIRECTIONS

1. Have students sit in a circle holding the rope in front of them with both hands.

2. On your command, the students attempt to stand while maintaining their grip on the rope.

⚠ SAFETY TIP

Please use the knot shown in figure 1.5 to ensure that it will not slip while students are attempting this activity. Remind students to take care of each other and that the goal is for the entire class to be successful.

TEACHING TIP

This is a difficult task if students are not coordinating their movements by applying equal pressure on the rope. Allow the students to problem solve this situation, which may take several attempts.

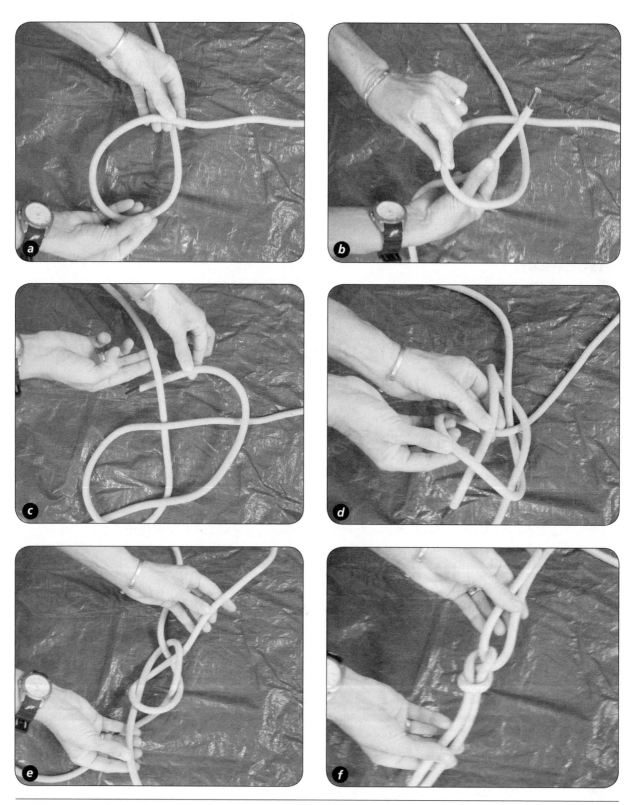

FIGURE 1.5 No-slip knot.

All Aboard

OBJECTIVES

Communication, teamwork

EQUIPMENT

1 tarp for every 12 students

SETUP

This activity should take place in an enclosed area so that students can hear well.

DIRECTIONS

1. Have students form groups of 12 and give each group a tarp.
2. When you call out, "All aboard!", students step on the tarp, ensuring that all body parts are on the tarp.
3. When all students are on the tarp, ask the students to step off the tarp and fold it in half.
4. Repeat the command, "All aboard!", with all students stepping on their folded tarp.
5. The process is repeated, with the tarp getting smaller and smaller. It becomes more difficult for all students to stand on the tarp as the area becomes smaller and smaller. Students must ensure that everyone is included and safe.

TEACHING TIPS

Ask debriefing questions such as the following:

1. Who emerged from the group as leaders? What did they say or how did they become the leaders of your group?
2. What made your group able to complete the activity?
3. Were there any conflicts within the group, and if so, how were they resolved? Was the group more successful when the problems were resolved?

Also keep in mind the following tips:

- There is no time limit for students to complete the task. The goal is group success rather than how quickly the task can be completed.
- Roam throughout the class, ensuring that groups are completely on the tarp and all body parts are on the tarp. Challenge students but make sure the situation is always safe.
- As the challenge increases, it becomes necessary for the group to communicate. Natural leaders will emerge, as will possible conflicts. Although you are monitoring interactions, it's important to allow the group dynamic to emerge.
- Share with students that their success is determined when everyone experiences success.

Shark Bait

OBJECTIVES

Communication, teamwork

EQUIPMENT

25 hula hoops

SETUP

Place hula hoops throughout the gym or designated area (i.e., ocean) as safe zones.

DIRECTIONS

1. Choose one student to be the shark. The other students are the fish. At your signal, the fish begin swimming (i.e., walking) around the ocean.
2. At your signal, the shark enters the ocean and tries to tag the fish. When the shark swims near, the fish must try to enter a hula hoop and encourage other fish to join them.
3. This is not a typical tag game—once students are tagged, they do not become a shark or sit out. To add excitement, have students put one arm behind their back or hop on one leg after being tagged.
4. At your signal, the shark leaves the ocean, and the fish resume swimming until the shark returns for another round. The key is to maintain a rapid pace, with the shark arriving and departing quickly so that students don't have time to be selective about who they join in the safe zones. After three or four repetitions, select another shark.

TEACHING TIP

Be sure to stress the safety of everyone who is a fish. Success is measured by everyone being safe and taking care of each other.

VARIATION

To make the activity more challenging, remove some hula hoops from the floor so the fish have fewer safe zones.

Eagle's Nest

OBJECTIVES

Dodging skills, cardiorespiratory fitness

EQUIPMENT

8 squares, 20 × 20 feet (6 × 6 meters) each; 8 foam noodles

SETUP

This activity requires an area approximately the size of a basketball court. Within the area, position the squares as shown. Place a noodle in each square. The ideal scenario has 8 eagles and 40 predators.

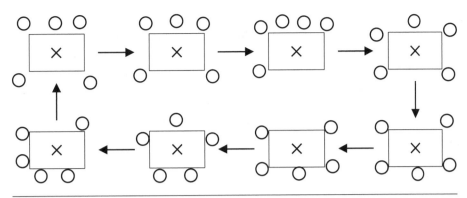

FIGURE 1.6 Eagle's Nest setup.

DIRECTIONS

1. Select students to be an eagle stationed in each of the nests (squares).

2. Evenly distribute the remaining students near each nest as predators.

3. The goal for the eagles is to remove all predators from their nest at any given time by tagging them with the noodle, whereas the goal for predators is to remain as long as possible in the nest of the eagle. When predators are tagged by an eagle, they must rotate to the next nest, where another eagle will attempt to tag and remove them.

4. The game continues until you end it. Gauge when to rotate new eagles into the game—usually students will remain engaged in this activity for 8 to 12 minutes.

TEACHING TIP

This is a continuous game where all students are participating at the same time. Although an eagle may have temporary relief from a predator, the predators will continue to arrive at the nest when they are tagged by the eagle from the previous nest.

Pipeline

OBJECTIVES

Cooperation, teamwork

EQUIPMENT

12-inch (30-centimeter) PVC pipes cut in half vertically to create two half-pipes (1 half-pipe per student), 1 marble per group, 1 bucket per group

SETUP

Place a bucket about 50 feet (15 meters) from each group of students.

DIRECTIONS

1. Place students in groups of 10 to 12. Each student has a pipe and each group has a marble.

2. Explain that students must work together to drop their marble in their bucket by rolling their marble along the pipeline without using their hands. To be successful,

students must place their individual pipe next to that of another student in their group to create a route for the marble to roll from point A to B.

3. The marble must roll along the pipe of each student. Because the marble moves quickly when the pipe is tilted, students must be patient and coordinate their movements to be successful.

4. The activity ends when the marble falls in the bucket. If the marble is dropped before reaching the bucket, the group must return to the starting point and begin again.

TEACHING TIPS

- Students will soon realize that they must develop good communication to achieve this task.
- Students will learn how to form a stable pipeline by moving from the back to the front of the line.
- This activity can become frustrating for some groups. Stress that it's not a race—success is completing the task in a manner that is respectful of all participants.

VARIATION

Tunnel It: Use flexible air vents to pass tennis balls to the bucket. Students must cooperate in order to manipulate the vents to send the tennis ball through the tube.

Affirmation Circle

OBJECTIVE

Respect

EQUIPMENT

1 balloon, 1 piece of paper, and 1 pencil per student

SETUP

This activity requires an indoor space, approximately the size of half a basketball court.

DIRECTIONS

1. Give each student a balloon, a small piece of paper, and a pencil.

2. Ask students to write an affirmation on the paper. The affirmation is something that they wish that someone would say to them, such as "You are a wonderful friend." The affirmation should begin with "You are . . . ."

3. Students fold the paper small enough to fit inside the balloon. Then they inflate the balloon, tie it off, and throw it into the center of the area.

4. Each person chooses a balloon from the pile.

5. The group forms two concentric circles of equal size so that all students have someone standing in front of them. Then they pop the balloon they have chosen and memorize the message on the paper.

6. On your signal, the people in the outer circle move clockwise around the circle and whisper their affirmation to each person in the inner circle. After a few minutes, participants switch positions and do the same for the new inner circle. Each student

in the outer circle repeats the message to every student within the inner circle. At the conclusion, every student in the inner circle will have heard every affirmation provided by the outer circle.

TEACHING TIPS

- This activity helps students build self-confidence.
- When sharing the affirmation, remind students to make it appropriate to the person to whom they are whispering if it is gender related (i.e., if the affirmation says, "You are a wonderful brother," change *brother* to *sister* if whispering to a girl).

Adapted from P. Allor and C. Eichelberger, *No One Is Left Out: Non-Traditional Games and Activities for Middle School Physical Education*.

Card Ranking

OBJECTIVES

Respect, tolerance

EQUIPMENT

Deck of cards

SETUP

Students are in an enclosed space and each receive a playing card.

DIRECTIONS

1. Students do not look at their playing card. They hold their card against their forehead so that others can see its value.
2. Students then mingle and greet each person based on the value of that person's card. High cards (face cards) are treated like royalty whereas low cards (ace, 2, 3) are not greeted as enthusiastically, if they are greeted at all. All other cards are greeted with different degrees of enthusiasm as related to their value.
3. After a couple of minutes, ask the students to stop mingling and line up from high to low. They cannot look at their card or reveal the value of other students' cards; instead, they must determine their ranking by how well they were treated by the group.

TEACHING TIPS

- The high and low cards will know immediately where to report, with the middle-value cards being a little confused. During the debriefing, ask people how they felt about the activity.
- In the beginning, students with low-value cards will participate enthusiastically, but over time they start to withdraw because they are unwilling to place themselves in a situation where they will be wounded. The negative or lukewarm comments are experiences that they are not willing to engage in. Use this as an opportunity for students to brainstorm what behaviors they need to adopt to create an environment where everyone cheers each other on and participates fully.

Classroom Temperature

OBJECTIVES

Self-awareness, effort, and reflection

EQUIPMENT

Large drawing of thermometer with degrees indicating certain feelings (e.g., 50 = "OK," 10 = "I'm having a bad day" or "I feel lousy")

SETUP

Post the thermometer somewhere in your area where students can easily reach it.

DIRECTIONS

Students sign in 1 or 2 days a week to let you know how they feel.

TEACHING TIP

It's important to validate how kids feel and to acknowledge that they are going to have good days and bad days. Sometimes kids having a bad day can interfere with the lesson, so why not deal with it? Students who are having a difficult day may only require acknowledgment and some sympathy from the teacher. This can also lead to more conversation between the student and teacher on how to address a problem that may not otherwise be revealed.

Adapted from P. Allor and C. Eichelberger, *No One Is Left Out: Non-Traditional Games and Activities for Middle School Physical Education.*

Half-Tennis-Ball Elbow Snatch

OBJECTIVES

Eye–hand coordination, progressive difficulty

EQUIPMENT

100 half tennis balls, canisters for storage

SETUP

This activity requires an enclosed area or well-contained space; teachers will prepare tennis balls by cutting them in half.

DIRECTIONS

1. Students extend one arm forward with the palm facing up. They then bend their arm, bringing their palm toward their shoulder.
2. Students place the half tennis ball on the forearm right above the elbow joint. The arm is now in the release mode.
3. When ready, they snap the arm forward and snatch the half tennis ball with their hand.

VARIATIONS

- Use the opposite arm.
- Use both arms simultaneously.
- Add a second tennis ball, then a third, a fourth, and a fifth to either or both arms.

Collective Tally

OBJECTIVES

Teamwork, group observation, cardiorespiratory fitness

EQUIPMENT

32 tennis balls, 8 hula hoops, 1 bucket

SETUP

Place a bucket with 32 balls in the middle of the playing area.

DIRECTIONS

1. Assign students to eight teams and assign two teams to each corner of the room. Teams stand behind their team hula hoop, facing the center.
2. On your command, teams send one student to retrieve a ball from either the center bucket or from another team's hula hoop. Students are not allowed to take balls from the team sharing their corner. Students cannot protect or guard against another team grabbing a ball out of their hula hoop.
3. Only one team member can leave the team at any given time. Once the student has retrieved a ball, the student tags another member to go. Students take turns leaving their area.
4. The game ends when a team has four balls in their hula hoop.

TEACHING TIP

Teams must be mindful of how many balls each team has in their hula hoop.

VARIATIONS

- Collect a tennis ball while dribbling a basketball.
- Place a time limit on the game. All teams continue playing until the end of the stipulated time.
- Conduct the activity using scooters.

Stock Market

OBJECTIVES

Cooperation, teamwork

EQUIPMENT

150 poly spots with assigned points, 8 beanbags, 1 large bucket

SETUP

This game is similar to Collective Tally but with a slightly different twist. Place the bucket in the center of the playing area. Scatter poly spots around the perimeter of the bucket. Designate points to the poly spots by either writing numbers on the spots or designating points by color. The spots that are farthest away are worth more points than those that are closer to the bucket.

DIRECTIONS

1. Assign students to eight teams and provide each team with a beanbag.
2. Students attempt to earn points by tossing their beanbag into a bucket. They can claim their points by retrieving their beanbag before picking up the poly spot. They place the spot into their team's hula hoop and it is then safe.
3. Teams can only send one student at a time to earn points. All students must go before another student can repeat a turn.
4. If a student from another team is able to make a bucket from the same poly spot before the first team is able to retrieve the spot, the first team loses the spot to the second team.
5. The game ends when there are no more poly spots left on the floor. The team with the most points wins the game.

Four-Letter Word

OBJECTIVES

Cooperation, problem solving, communication, teamwork

EQUIPMENT

1 lettered index card per student

SETUP

Write a letter of the alphabet on each card, making enough cards so that there is at least one per student (it's a good idea to make a few extras). You may want to make a few cards with asterisks (*) on them, which are wild cards and can be used as any letter. For larger groups, make more cards with vowels and common consonants (such as s, d, m, l, and so on). Once you've made the cards, save them so they can be used again.

DIRECTIONS

1. Give each student a card. This is their letter for the duration of the activity.

2. On your signal, each player has 1 minute to find three other players who have letters that will spell a four-letter word (no swear words, obviously!). Before beginning, give a few examples, such as *frog, wild, rain,* and *team.*

3. Once four people have created a four-letter word, they stand together with their hands in the air.

4. After 1 minute, everyone stops where they are. If you are working with a large group, you may want to use a whistle or some other loud noisemaker (foghorns work well).

5. Quickly ask some of the groups what words they came up with. It's fun to see some of the words, and it recognizes people for their hard work.

6. Give groups 1 minute to introduce themselves to each other before finding new members to make new words. Players can think of something of interest to share about themselves that rhymes with their name or a word that starts with the first letter of their first name (e.g., Marvelous Mary, Babbling Bob), or players can state where they are from or what they like to eat.

7. After a short time of introductions, a new round begins and students look for three new people to form a new four-letter word.

8. Play five to eight rounds so that everyone has a good chance to form at least one four-letter word.

9. Players who are not able to get into a word group must find each other. Sometimes, students may have letters where they are unable to form a word. Have some fun and ask a nonword group to create an imaginary word from their letters and share a definition of the word with the class.

Adapted, by permission, from Youth Leaders, 1995, *Youth Leadership In Action, A Guide to Cooperative Games and Group Activities* (Beverly, MA: Project Adventure Inc.), 92.

Hi, How Are You? Gotta Go

OBJECTIVES

Getting to know other students, communication, self-esteem

EQUIPMENT

None

SETUP

This activity requires a well-contained space.

DIRECTIONS

1. Students walk up to fellow classmates, shake their hands, and introduce themselves.

2. Next, students give the way-cool introduction. They shake hands regularly, and then wrap fingers around the base of their partner's thumb, leaving thumbs interlocked. Finally, without disconnecting thumbs, they wave goodbye. While they are doing this, they say "Hi" (with regular handshake), "How are you?" (with interlocked thumbs), and "Gotta go" (with thumbs connected and waving goodbye).

TEACHING TIP

This makes for a fun introductory activity.

Thumb Wrestling

OBJECTIVES

Cooperation, getting to know other students, appropriate touching

EQUIPMENT

None

SETUP

Before beginning the activity, demonstrate how to thumb wrestle.

DIRECTIONS

1. Place students in partners.
2. Partners interlock the fingers of their right hands, thumbs pointing up. They say, "One, two, three, four, I declare a thumb war," while at the same time thumbs volley from side to side. Then they try to pin their thumb over their partner's thumb.
3. Students will initiate their own thumb wrestling matches and complete the best out of three. Then they find a new partner.

VARIATIONS

- Thumb wrestle with the left hand.
- Cross arms and wrestle both hands at the same time.

Courtesy Tag

OBJECTIVE

Politeness

EQUIPMENT

1 flag football belt and flag per student

SETUP

This activity requires a well-contained, designated space approximately the size of a tennis court.

DIRECTIONS

1. All students have a belt with one flag.
2. On your signal, students try to pull the flags from each other while not losing their own flag.

3. Students whose flags are pulled must put one knee on the ground and wait for another student to bring them a flag. The kneeling position is a safe position for students to put flags back on teammates—their flag can't be pulled while they're kneeling. Students can't kneel for safety if they are not being courteous and putting a flag on another student's belt.

4. Once the students have pulled their first flag, they must give the flag to someone who is kneeling before they can pull a flag from someone else.

5. Students continue to play until time is called. Students will usually stay engaged for 8 to 12 minutes.

TEACHING TIP

Students will realize that in order to play, they must help their classmates.

Random Count

OBJECTIVES

Listening skills, group cohesion, timing, anticipation

EQUIPMENT

None

SETUP

This activity requires a well-defined space approximately the size of half a basketball court.

DIRECTIONS

1. Place students in groups of 5 to 7.

2. Each group must count from 1 to 15. The group may not develop a strategy on how to accomplish the task before starting, nor can they communicate during the activity. They must use and develop nonverbal means to communicate so that they can successfully accomplish the task. A student within each group initiates the count by calling out, "One." The goal is for the group to count from 1 to 15 by having one member call out a number and another call out the next number until reaching 15.

3. If more than one student calls out a number at the same time, the group must start over. Students also cannot call out more than one number in a row.

TEACHING TIP

Ask students what strategies they were able to develop or create during the activity. How were they able to accomplish the task?

VARIATIONS

- Count from 1 to 25.
- Count odd numbers from 1 to 25.
- Count even numbers from 2 to 24.
- Time it.

Half the Feet

OBJECTIVES

Strategy, verbal communication, trial and error, appropriate touch

EQUIPMENT

None

SETUP

This activity requires a well-defined area about the length of a basketball court.

DIRECTIONS

1. Line students up and place them in groups of 2, 4, or 6.
2. Students must work together to move as a group across the court only using half the number of legs in their group. Some possible solutions might be for half of the students to roll while half walk, or for each student to hop on one leg.

TEACHING TIP

This activity can be done after students have successfully completed initiatives such as All Aboard, Shark Bait, and so on that allow them to be comfortable with appropriate touch and problem-solving techniques.

Math Face-Off

OBJECTIVE

Improve thinking reaction time

EQUIPMENT

None

SETUP

This activity requires a well-defined area about the length of a basketball court. Before beginning the activity, demonstrate how students should hold up any number of fingers from 0 to 10 when you call out "Face off."

DIRECTIONS

1. Instruct students to select a partner and face their partner at half-court, hands behind their back.
2. When you say, "One, two, three, face off," the students bring their hands forward and flash a number between 0 and 10 using their fingers.
3. Students try to be the first person to yell out the number of fingers the other person is holding up.

TEACHING TIPS

- This activity requires a great deal of concentration.
- Continue with the variations to incorporate some cardiorespiratory work into the activity.

VARIATIONS

- Students try to add up the total number of fingers both players are holding up. Designate one student as odd and the other as even. If the sum of the numbers is odd, the odd student tries to tag the even student before the even student reaches the end line. If the sum is even, the even student tries to tag the odd student. Students must try to reach the line behind them before they are tagged. Students return to the center and they play again.
- Students try to find the product of both numbers by multiplying them.

Mystical Wave

OBJECTIVES

Trust, teamwork, creating a positive learning environment

EQUIPMENT

None

SETUP

This activity requires a well-defined area.

DIRECTIONS

1. Students form two lines facing each other.
2. Select a student to walk between the two lines.
3. As the walkers pass the students in the lines, they raise their hands and cheer, creating a wave.

TEACHING TIP

As simple as this seems, students love to walk through the alley of students cheering them on. The purpose is to send positive, affirming messages to students.

VARIATIONS

- Send the student through running.
- Send several students through at the same time.

Fitness Made Fun

> **"N**one are so old as those who have outlived enthusiasm."
>
> —*Henry David Thoreau*

Many years ago, I used to have students run a mile (1.5 kilometers) during one class a week. I felt I was doing what was best for them by training their hearts and strengthening their muscles. However, I soon noticed a pattern—I'd receive an unusually high number of notes from parents excusing their child from physical education every Thursday, which just happened to be the fitness day! So I began to change fitness days without notifying the students, sometimes holding it on a Monday, another week on a Wednesday. I thought I had them fooled, but soon I began to receive a flood of notes with suspicious parent signatures by the end of a fitness day.

I was sharing my dilemma with a friend, criticizing the parents and students for not supporting physical education, when she said, "Why would they want to participate? What joy is there in running around a track for 20 minutes? What's fun about running on a treadmill?" That's when it hit me. Physical education for me is about fun, yet I was not providing fun experiences for my students. That's when I asked myself, "How can I make physical activity fun again and teach students to play?"

We have heard it said many times that yesterday was different than today, and this is certainly the case when we examine how active children were 15 years ago compared with children today. Children from days gone by entertained themselves through move-ment—riding a bike, throwing a ball, chasing or fleeing. The only virtual reality they possessed was acted out in play from their imagination. MOOMBA was alive and well. There were no obstacles that prevented us from chasing the bad guys, racing our horses, or flying to the moon. We used our physical bodies combined with our imaginations to move mountains. Our bodies were integrated in our play.

This kind of movement motivated many children to continue with physical activity because of the interaction with others, the world around them, and the challenges they faced. I remember as a child running like the wind to chase my friends. We tugged and jumped and moved. We did not have rules, and there were no winners or losers—our play was for the pure joy of movement.

With the easy accessibility of video games, television, and similar entertainment, children today do not need to move to engage in social behaviors. Most children live sedentary lives, which is resulting in an epidemic of obesity, diabetes, hypertension, and heart disease. As physical educators, we must ask ourselves what we can do to re-create the joy of movement that is within each child. Is it not our professional duty, our moral responsibility to provide experiences that will help children develop a joy in movement? MOOMBA returns us to that moment when play was central.

This chapter presents fun activities to motivate, challenge, and get students excited about fitness. Students will learn about health-related fitness components (cardiorespi-ratory fitness, body composition, muscular strength, endurance, and flexibility) and skill-related fitness components (agility, balance, coordination, power, and speed). The activities are fun and appropriate for all students regardless of fitness level.

Through the activities in this chapter, hopefully you'll discover that fitness can be fun for students. They will not only enjoy the activities, but they will also learn how to play, run, chase, and laugh while their hearts beat with joy.

Incentives

Incentives and recognition programs for student achievement and improvement not only challenge students to improve their fitness level but also help them to establish goals. A good recognition program gives all students an opportunity to be recognized. Here are some ideas that can help you create that kind of program.

Full Status

100 sit-ups in 2 minutes

10 pull-ups

Elite Runner status

75 push-ups in 4 minutes

Junior Status

50 sit-ups in 2 minutes

5 pull-ups

Elite Runner status

50 push-ups in 4 minutes

FIGURE 2.1   Full versus junior status.

Elite Runner

Students can earn Elite Runner status by arranging to test their endurance in a mile (1.5-kilometer) run. A standard time is posted so it is well known by students, such as 6:30 for boys and 7:30 for girls. Times can be adjusted to your school or situation. Students who earn elite status receive a certificate, a patch that can be ironed onto their uniform, and their picture and time placed on the wall of fame. (See reproducible 2.1, "Elite Runner Status," on the CD-ROM.)

Fitness Entrance Exam

Students can attempt to complete a fitness entrance exam that is given to potential firefighters, police officers, and even government agents. This is a fun way to allow students to make a connection between a profession and its fitness requirements. You can select any organization that pertains to your geographical location. A firefighter or police officer can visit the class and share with students the fitness requirements of the department and even train with them. Students can attempt to earn junior status or full status, depending on how much of the exam they're able to complete; see figure 2.1 for examples. On the CD-ROM, you'll find the scoring scale for those seeking to become special agents at the Federal Bureau of Investigation (FBI) (reproducible 2.2, "FBI Special Agent Physical Fitness Test Scoring Scale").

If possible, hold a ceremony at the conclusion of the training time (6 months or so), where the guest officer awards certificates to the students who successfully completed the program.

Improvement Recognition

Every 6 weeks, give students bonus points, certificates, or iron-on patches for improved performance. Goals could include any component of fitness. The focus is on improvement, not the skill level or score attained by the student. The recognition could be for 10 percent improvement, 20 percent improvement, and so on.

Fitness Record Sheet

Teachers keep records of times and number of repetitions during the year for curl-ups, crunches, mile run, and so on. Post results for students who attained the best time or the highest number of repetitions during the year.

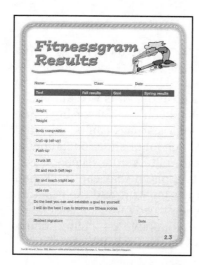

Fitnessgram Assessment

This form allows students to record their fitness pre- and posttest results. Use the form to help students establish goals. Save the students' forms for the year for them, and remember to revisit the goals to help motivate students to apply themselves during physical activity. (See reproducible 2.3, "Fitnessgram Results," on the CD-ROM.)

Running Self-Score

This form allows students to reflect on how much effort they exert in their play. Use it from time to time to train students to be aware of their effort and how it affects their score. (See reproducible 2.4, "Running Program Assessment," on the CD-ROM.)

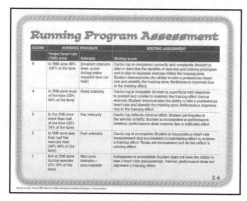

Clubs and Special Events

Sponsor a club or special event that encourages students to participate in active daily movement. For example, you could sponsor clubs for hiking, wall climbing, walking, tennis, or other fitness-related activities. As for special events, be creative! For example, the physical education department at our school sponsored a medieval game fair where faculty members dressed in costumes and engaged students in games or challenges. This event occurred during lunch time and included a lunch and music for students who participated. The cost to students was minimal and included a lunch provided by a local restaurant recruited to sponsor the event (scholarships were available for students on free and reduced lunch). The raised funds were used to purchase fitness equipment for the department.

Just Play Activity Log

Encourage students to be active beyond the school day, and encourage parents to participate with their children in an active lifestyle through the Just Play Activity Log. Most students are sedentary because their family does not engage in activity on a daily basis. Family fitness nights provide an opportunity for physical educators, nurses, and other health professionals to meet with families and provide information about the benefits of and need for daily activity. Parents receive information about nutrition, exercise, and options for family activities. The key component is to encourage the students to participate in activity with adults or peers, helping them to develop a healthy, active lifestyle. (See reproducible 2.5, "Just Play Activity Log," on the CD-ROM.)

Success and Fun for All

When designing a fitness component within the physical education curriculum, it's important that activities are fun and student centered and that they differentiate among student fitness levels. Do not grade students on whether they are able to attain a certain percentage of a national physical fitness norm. Rather, assess how much students have improved throughout the year, recognizing the work invested in their personal fitness.

Cardio Days

Students need variety to stay engaged in an aerobic fitness program. Time is not the sole factor in assessing how hard a student is working; heart rate is a better indicator. Monitoring exercise heart rate is central to an aerobic fitness program; thus traditional fitness runs with grades determined by time should not be the basis for fitness grades in physical education. Although you should provide attention and recognition for students who need to be challenged, assessments of achievement should be based on maximization of students' individual aerobic capacity.

Although fitness and strength are integral to most activities you will provide throughout the year, consider setting aside a day each week specifically for aerobic exercise in order to develop cardiorespiratory fitness. On these days, focus on training within students' target zone for at least 20 minutes. Students will learn how to determine their heart rate and record beats per minute on their cardio log, a record of performance for each cardio workout. (Students only need to fill out the cardio log a couple of times per semester to chart their progress. The specific dates for charting will be determined by the teacher.) They will also learn about resting, exercise, recovery, and target heart rates, as well as the training zone. Finally, they will begin to understand how effort directly affects improvements in cardiorespiratory fitness.

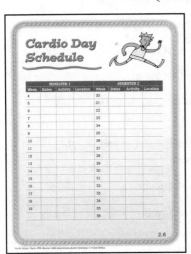

Cardio days should be fun and interesting. Students will look forward to seeing what activity is waiting to challenge them. (See figure 2.2 and reproducibles 2.6, "Cardio Day Schedule," and 2.7, "Cardio Log," on the CD-ROM.)

Half-Mile Instructional Run

A pretest is one way to assess students' fitness levels and the effectiveness of training programs. The purpose of the half-mile (1-kilometer) instructional run is to instruct students on basic skills to monitor and record performance. Students learn how to assess their work load and performance, as well as how to chart their performance in the cardio log through heart rate, time, and distance. Before the half-mile run, students learn how to take and record their heart rate; they learn about resting, exercise, and recovery heart rates; and they practice the correct technique.

Resting Heart Rate

Students record their resting heart rate, or the number of beats per minute during rest, by placing their second and third fingers of their right hand on their right carotid artery (see figure 2.3). The students count the beats for 30 seconds and then multiply by 2 (the first beat is counted as 0). Resting heart rates are only recorded in the cardio log each semester or quarter.

Semester 1				Semester 2			
Week	Dates	Activity	Location	Week	Dates	Activity	Location
4	Sept. 25	Short Circuits	Gym	20	Jan. 29	Math on the Move	MR
5	Oct. 2	Tire Run	Track	21	Feb. 5	Trio Tag; Teeter-Totter Tag	Field
6	Oct. 9	Monarchy Versus Anarchy	Gym	22	Feb. 12	Mosquito Tag	MR
7	Oct. 16	Pass the Fat Tag	Gym	23	Feb. 19	Boneyard Scrabble	MR
8	Oct. 23	Clothespin Tag; Foot-Pass Train	Gym	24	Feb. 26	Two-Ball Challenge	Gym
9	Oct. 30	Cat and Mouse	Gym	25	Mar. 4	Knights Unite	Field
10	Nov. 6	Two-Ball Challenge	Gym	26	Mar. 11	Beehives	Field
11	Nov. 13	Smokers Tag	Gym	27	Mar. 18	Krazy Kones	MR
12	Nov. 20	Ultimate Soccer	Gym	28	Mar. 25	Fitness Scrabble	MR
13	Nov. 27	Eurofoam Mania	MR	29	Apr. 1	My Last Breath	Track
14	Dec. 4	Ultimate Hockey	Gym	30	Apr. 22	My Last Breath	Track
15	Dec. 11	Teeter-Totter Tag	Gym	31	Apr. 29	Smokers Tag; Push-Up Toss	Gym
16	Dec. 18	Roundup	Gym	32	May 6	Triangle Tag; Cat and Mouse	MR
17	Jan. 8	Balance Tag; Trio Tag	Gym	33	May 13	Short Circuits	Track
18	Jan. 15	Spin Tag; Rock, Paper, Scissors	Gym	34	May 20	Cone Savers	Tennis court
19	Jan. 22	Krazy Kones	Gym	35	May 27	Pop or Be Popped	MR
				36	June 3	Push-Up Toss Up and Over	MR

MR = multipurpose room

FIGURE 2.2 Sample cardio day schedule.

Exercise Heart Rate

Students must master the ability to take their exercise heart rate, or the number of beats per minute during peak exercise, since rates dramatically decrease when exercise ceases. Immediately after exercise, they take their heart rate for 6 seconds and multiply by 10. The recorded heart rate has a margin of error of 20 beats (since a 1-beat miscount is multiplied by 10), so students should take a 20-second count and multiply by 3 to increase accuracy. Because the heart rate recovers to the resting rate quickly in fit people, the quicker the student is able to measure a heart rate after the cessation of exercise, the more accurate the results.

FIGURE 2.3 A student takes the resting heart rate from her right carotid artery.

Recovery Heart Rate

One minute after exercise, students record their recovery heart rate on the Cardio Log. Students take their heart rate for 20 seconds and multiply the results by 3.

Structuring Lessons

A successful cardio lesson has a lot of variety at a fast pace. The mistake many teachers make is staying with an activity so long that students' fatigue and boredom have a negative effect on engagement. Many of the activities in this chapter do not require much setup or equipment so that students can move freely from grouping to grouping—singles, partners, small groups, large groups, and so on. In time, students will know how to get into a group quickly and will become familiar enough with certain activities to immediately move into a particular formation. Training students well thus helps maximize movement time.

The activities on pages 48 through 50 are brief movement activities that focus on a particular fitness component. Those on pages 52 through 75 are whole-class activities that keep students engaged and moving. You should use the larger activities at least once a week, and you can supplement them with any of the shorter, focused-fitness activities.

Putting It Together

Following are sample activities used in combination for a training effect. Activities are fast paced and sequential, and they allow for specificity within a targeted fitness area (cardiovascular, aerobic, abdominal, muscular, and so on).

The focused-fitness activities on pages 48 to 50 are designed to be used in a series or combination of several activities during one class with 27 minutes of movement time. Students are paired and follow your instructions. Although the partner strength activities are listed as 2 to 3 minutes, keep the pace moving by having students perform the task for only 15 seconds and allowing about 15 seconds for students to recover from the activity. They then resume the activity and continue the cycle until they have completed four to six matches. Then you can signal them to move to the next activity.

Notice the lesson begins with a whole-group activity and ends with a whole-group activity. This provides a time of closure during which you can praise student achievement, encourage positive choices, and end on a positive note.

An example of a lesson sequence could be the following:

1. Four Corners: Whole-class warm-up (4 minutes)
2. Push-Up Toss: Partner upper-body exercise (2-3 minutes, 15-second intervals)
3. Push-Up Snatch: Partner upper-body exercise (2-3 minutes, 15-second intervals)
4. Curl-Up Toss: Partner abdominal exercise (2-3 minutes, 15-second intervals)
5. Snatch and Grab: Partner abdominal exercise (2-3 minutes, 15-second intervals)
6. Can Pass: Group abdominal exercise (4 minutes)
7. Rock, Paper, Scissors: Whole-group aerobic exercise (4 minutes)

Following is another example of a sample lesson:

1. Four Corners (4 minutes)
2. Push-Up Toss (2-3 minutes)
3. Curl-Up Toss (2-3 minutes)
4. Any Fitness Made Fun activity from this chapter (15 minutes)

Note that students can perform the push-up activities using any of these positions:

1. Both knees with hands extended
2. One knee down, one leg extended
3. Both legs extended with full body weight on the arms

Individual Activities

These activities allow students to challenge themselves and reach personal goals. They can be incorporated before or after a partner or group activity as a warm-up or closure within a day's lesson. To keep students motivated, have them keep a journal on how much they have improved or challenge them to better their previous performance. Keep the activity short, in no more than 15- to 20-second intervals, and change the activity after two or three repetitions. Variety, change of pace, quick transitions, challenges, and encouragement keep the students engaged.

Ball Taps

Students are in the push-up position. Put a basketball between their hands. Students alternate tapping the ball with the right and left hands without moving the ball. They count how many times they can tap the ball for 15 seconds. They rest for 15 seconds and then begin again. Do three sets.

Variations

- Students roll the ball from the right to left hands.
- Students toss the ball from the right to left hands. (They must try to catch the ball with the opposite hand while maintaining a push-up position.)

Roll Around

While maintaining a push-up position with one hand, students roll the ball around that hand. Next, they try a figure-eight pattern, alternating hands.

Push-Up Ball Touches

Students do a push-up and attempt to drop to the level of the ball by touching the ball with their forehead. Students can use balls of several different sizes to challenge themselves.

Partner Activities

Partner activities are just plain fun. Working with a partner or group to achieve a task focuses students' attention on the goal of the activity. Many students will apply more effort to accomplish the task while working with a partner than if required to complete the task alone. Students can select their own partners initially, but have students change partners often throughout the lesson. Many of these activities do not require partners to have similar size or strength, so there is great flexibility in how students are paired.

The partner activities are adapted from J. Hichwa, *Right fielders are people too: An inclusive approach to teaching middle school physical education* (Champaign, IL: Human Kinetics).

"Partner Ball Exchange" and "Partner Squat and Push-Up" on pages 54 and 55 describe two other partner activities.

Push-Up Toss

Students are placed in pairs, facing each other in a push-up position. One partner has a beanbag in one hand and tosses the bag to the other student, who attempts to catch it.

Push-Up Toss Up and Over

One person is in the push-up position while the other student stands behind at the feet. Students in the push-up position have a beanbag in front of them. On your signal, they toss the bag over their shoulder so that their partners can catch it. The students in the push-up position then complete one push-up and their partners replace the beanbag in front of them. Repeat for a designated time or number of reps.

Push-Up Snatch

Place a beanbag between two partners facing each other in a push-up position. On your signal, they try to steal the bag before the other person does, all while remaining in a push-up position.

Push-Up Hockey or Soccer

Partners face each other in a push-up position. The students have a beanbag between them. One student tries to slide the beanbag through the other student's arms to score a goal. The other student tries to block the object with one hand while remaining in the push-up position. The beanbag alternates between partners.

Dice Push-Ups

Form groups of 2 or 3 students and give each group a die. Students roll their die and perform that number of push-ups. You could also use a deck of cards, with each number indicating the number of push-ups required.

Three-Person Challenge

Three people face each other in a push-up position. One person does one push-up, then the next person does one, and then the third person does one. Next, the first student completes two push-ups while the others maintain their push-up position, then the second student completes two push-ups, and finally the third student completes two push-ups. The first student then attempts three push-ups, and so on. Students continue until they can no longer complete a sequence. Once students have exhausted their attempts, they rest for 15 seconds and go again.

Snatch and Grab

Students are in pairs in curl-up position. They lie on the ground with their feet interlaced, the top of each foot placed behind the partner's calf with the heel pressed to the floor. A beanbag is resting to one side of the pair. They curl up as many times as they can during a specific amount of time, approximately 10 seconds, and on a signal from you, they try to grab the beanbag before the other person grabs it. On another signal, they place the beanbag back in its resting place and continue to perform curl-ups until the signal is sounded again to grab the beanbag.

Group Activities

Group activities allow for greater individual recovery time within the workout session, so students can spend more time on a task. But the real strength of group activities is the re-creation of the MOOMBA effect. Students focus on encouraging one another and contributing to the group performance. It is very important that we focus not on how quickly a group can complete a task but on how well a group can accomplish its goal.

Students will tend to compare their group effort to another group, so it is important when we, as teachers, initially introduce group activities that we redirect their focus to another variation of the task or help students discuss amongst themselves how they can improve their group performance.

"Foot-Pass Train" on page 56 is another fun group activity that focuses on teamwork.

Can Pass

Place students in groups of 6 to 8. Students sit in a circle shoulder to shoulder with their legs extended toward the center of the circle. They pass an empty coffee can or paint can around the circle from student to student using only their feet. When students are in possession of the can, their legs must not touch the ground.

Variations

- See how quickly the group can pass the can around the circle.
- See how many times the group can pass the can around the circle.

Short Circuits

Short circuits allow students to meet fitness challenges in a fun, supportive environment. Students experience a series of activities that work different parts of the body or different components of fitness. The amount of time and number of stations can vary depending on the day's activities. Figure 2.4 shows a sample activity. The CD-ROM contains a total of 20 short circuit activities. (See reproducible 2.9, "Short Circuits," on the CD-ROM.)

Full-Game Activities

We know through experience that it is difficult to motivate students to sustain movement using traditional methods of developing fitness: running around a track or doing push-ups, sit-ups, and jumping jacks. The activities on pages 57 through 75 provide a motivator by engaging students in games with a goal. Students can't help but be fully involved in these games. Because of the novelty of these activities, students are open to engaging in them. They are fun and help develop fitness. Incorporate these activities at least once a week. You can use any of the focused-fitness activities listed previously to complement them.

Short Circuit 1

Sit-Up Wars

1. Find a partner.
2. Face each other in sit-up position.
3. Pick up the deck of cards and split it in half.
4. Perform a sit-up and place the top card by your feet.
5. The player with the highest card takes both cards. If both players place cards of the same value, each player should place three cards facedown on the ground. The fourth card determines who will take all cards on the ground.
6. Repeat.

Keep playing until someone has all the cards or until you rotate to the next station.

2.9a

From M. Hirt and I. Ramos, 2008, *Maximum middle school physical education* (Champaign, IL: Human Kinetics).

FIGURE 2.4 Sample short circuit activity.

Four Corners

OBJECTIVE

Warm-up

EQUIPMENT

Four Corners signs, 4 cones

SETUP

This movement is a warm-up for the class; students begin the activity quickly with little direct instruction from you. Set up the cones to define the corners of a square or rectangle about the size of a basketball half-court, and place one sign on each of the four cones (you can print the signs; see reproducible 2.8, the Four Corners signs, on the CD-ROM).

DIRECTIONS

1. Divide the class into groups of four and assign each group to a corner cone.
2. Blow a whistle to begin the activity. All students do the movement shown on the sign in their corner while traveling to the next corner. Students then switch to the movement shown on the new sign and travel to the next corner.
3. Students move around the four corners for 6 to 10 minutes.

TEACHING TIPS

After a few rotations, debrief with students using the following questions:

- What muscle groups were used in each section?
- Which was most demanding? Why?

VARIATION

Change the movement patterns often and be creative. The signs on the CD-ROM include skipping, jogging, bear crawling, and crab walking, but you can make your own signs that depict side steps, lunges, grapevines, and so on.

Math on the Move

OBJECTIVES

Reaction time, fleeing, cardiorespiratory endurance

EQUIPMENT

None

SETUP

This activity requires an area the length of a basketball court. Create a well-defined space with a center line and safety zones approximately 50 feet (15 meters) from each side of the center line. Before class begins, prepare 10 to 15 mathematical problems whose answers result in whole numbers.

DIRECTIONS

1. Divide the class into two groups and partner them. Designate one partner as odd and the other as even.
2. Students face each other at the center line.
3. Read a math problem. Students solve the problem and determine if the answer is odd or even.
4. If the answer is odd, the odd students are It and try to tag their partners before they reach the safety zone on their side of the court. If the answer is even, the even students are It.
5. When a runner is tagged or reaches the safety zone, both partners return to the center line.
6. After all students have returned to the center line, read another math problem.

VARIATIONS

- Rock, Paper, Scissors: Instead of a math problem, students use Rock, Paper, Scissors (see page 21 in chapter 1) to determine who is It. Students do not wait for your cue to begin. Movement is continuous until stopped by you.
- Math Face-Off: Students use the initial Rock, Paper, Scissors motions but hold up any number of fingers on both hands. The students must add or multiply the fingers from both partners to determine if the sum is odd or even (see page 38).
- Pass Tag: Partners face each other across the center line and begin tossing a foam ball to each other. When the music stops, whoever has the ball is the tagger and the other student is the runner.

Partner Ball Exchange

OBJECTIVES

Abdominal strength, flexibility, timing

EQUIPMENT

25 soft objects

SETUP

This activity requires a well-defined space; if on a hard surface, have mats available for students.

DIRECTIONS

1. Students partner up and get an object.
2. They sit down facing each other with knees bent and soles of the feet touching their partner's soles.
3. Students toss the object to their partner when they curl up. They return to the down position and repeat for approximately 15 to 20 seconds. Students stop and rest for approximately 10 seconds and repeat another set. Students see how many tosses they can accomplish within each repetition and add how many they can accomplish for their set score. Try three sets, rest for 15 seconds, and repeat a second set.

VARIATIONS

- See how many exchanges partners can do in 10 seconds.
- See how quickly partners can exchange the ball 10 times.
- Curl-Up Toss: After two catches, both students move back one body length. After two more catches, they move back another body length, and so on. How far back can they get in 30 seconds?
- In groups of four, students pass the ball to the right until everyone has received it. They try to pass as many times as they can for 30 seconds. Then they try passing the ball to the left.

Partner Squat and Push-Up

OBJECTIVES

Teamwork, balance, cooperation, push-ups, squats

EQUIPMENT

25 soft objects or balls

SETUP

This activity requires a well-defined space and enough objects for every partner to have one.

DIRECTIONS

1. Students partner up, get an object, and face each other.
2. They pin the ball or object between their foreheads, squat together, and then stand without dropping it.

VARIATIONS

- See how many times partners can squat and stand without letting their ball hit the ground.
- See how quickly pairs can squat and stand.
- Partners attempt to squat, kick their legs out and bring them in, and stand without dropping the ball.
- Partners attempt to squat, kick their legs out, do a push-up, bring their legs in, and stand together without letting the ball hit the ground.

Foot-Pass Train

OBJECTIVE

Teamwork

EQUIPMENT

1 Gator Ball or soft object for every 5 or 6 students, 10 cones

SETUP

This activity requires an area approximately the size of a basketball court. Place cones to mark where students begin the activity and at the end line.

DIRECTIONS

1. Place students in groups of 5 or 6. Each group sits on the floor in a line, side by side.

2. The first person in each group places a ball or object between the feet. On the go signal, the first player exchanges the ball with the next player's feet. The players use only their feet to make the exchange.

3. After the exchange, the first person goes to the end of the line, sits, and waits for the ball to arrive for the next turn to pass.

4. Each person repeats the sequence as fast as possible until the group reaches its designated area. If the ball is dropped, the group must start over at the beginning.

Cone Savers

OBJECTIVES

Strategy, communication, accuracy, cardiorespiratory endurance

EQUIPMENT

25 yellow cones, 25 orange cones, 60 Eurofoam or tennis balls, 8 scooters, 2 ropes (length will vary, depending on the width of the court), 8 trash-can lids

SETUP

Divide a tennis court in half. In the middle of the court, set up two parallel lines of 25 cones each. Each line of cones should be approximately 20 feet (6 meters) from the court baseline. Secure a rope along the baselines so that it spans the width of the court, using a secure knot (see figure 2.5) and a carabiner.

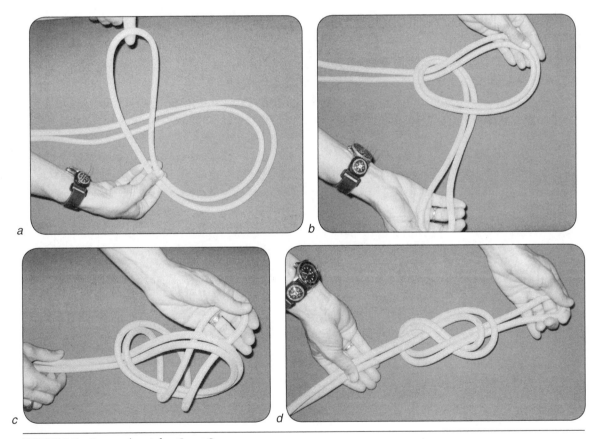

FIGURE 2.5 Secure knot for Cone Savers.

DIRECTIONS

1. Divide the class into two teams. Each team lines up slightly behind the assigned baseline, facing the center.
2. Each team has 30 tennis balls, which players will throw at the opposing team's cones on your signal. Teams must remain behind the baseline when throwing balls.
3. Within each team are four students who are designated as cone savers. Sitting on scooters, the cone savers pull themselves across the width of their end zone using a rope that's tied securely to the fence.
4. Once cone savers have moved from one side of the end zone to the other, they are eligible to leave their scooter, run into the center of the court, and reset one of their team's fallen cones. During this time, they use the trash-can lid as a shield.
5. Cone savers can only reset one cone at a time. After doing so, the cone savers join the rest of their team behind their baseline, and new students become the cone savers. Repeat steps 4 and 5 throughout the game.
6. The game is continuous, but the teacher gauges when to stop (or change cone savers, if necessary). After a quick debriefing (see Teaching Tips), the game starts again.

TEACHING TIPS

- This activity requires accuracy and power in throwing and communication in building a strategy to maintain point control.
- Between games, debrief with students using the following questions: What is going well? What can you improve? Talk to teammates to develop a strategy.

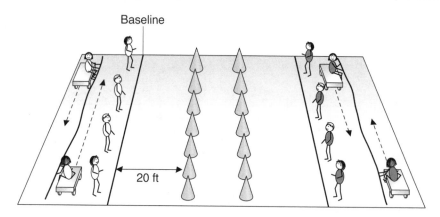

Baseline

20 ft

Tire Run

OBJECTIVES

Cardiorespiratory fitness, eye–hand coordination

EQUIPMENT

8-10 car tires, 6 cones

SETUP

Each cone represents a station. Place the cones to create a loop of the desired size. The bigger the loop, the greater the distance between stations.

DIRECTIONS

1. Divide the class into teams of six. Place one student from each team at each station.
2. Place the tires at station 1. When the activity begins, the students at station 1 roll or carry their tire to their teammate at station 2, passing it like a baton in a relay race.
3. The students who received the tire then roll or carry it to station 3 and pass it on to the next teammate, and so on. Continue the activity for 12 to 17 minutes.

VARIATION

Form teams of eight, placing two students at station 1 and two at station 3, and play with eight tires. Begin by having one student from station 1 and from station 3 carrying or rolling the tire to the next station. This creates shorter recovery time between intervals.

Clothespin Tag

OBJECTIVES

Dodging, fleeing, agility

EQUIPMENT

5-10 clothespins per student (the spring type that grips tightly)

SETUP

Spread students out in an area with clear boundaries. A smaller area (the size of a basketball half-court) means more action and enjoyment. Demonstrate how to appropriately place a clothespin on the bottom of a student's shirt without pinching the skin.

DIRECTIONS

1. Provide each student with five pins. Explain that the goal is to have the fewest pins possible when the activity is done.
2. On your signal, students begin placing pins on each other's shirts, being careful not to pinch the skin. Students can remove pins placed on them or pick up pins that have fallen to the floor to place on other students' shirts.
3. After 10 minutes, stop the activity and let the students recover for 1 minute.
4. Instruct students to collect all the pins in 2 minutes and turn them in to you.

TEACHING TIPS

- Students may only place pins on the bottom of the shirt or on the sleeves.
- Students cannot push players away.

VARIATIONS

- Students start with the clothespins on their clothing. The object is to not have their pins removed. There is no guarding pins with hands.
- Divide students into teams of 2 to 4. The object is for team members to work together to get rid of their pins. Students can take a moment to develop a strategy.

Roundup

OBJECTIVES

Cardiorespiratory endurance, dodging, fleeing, agility

EQUIPMENT

4-6 pinnies, 4-6 foam noodles

SETUP

This activity requires two adjacent basketball courts.

DIRECTIONS

1. Assign six students to be gobblers, and give each a pinny and a noodle.
2. Assign three gobblers to each court. The remainder of the class is divided evenly between the courts.
3. On your signal, the gobblers try to tag the other students by touching them gently with their noodle. A tagged student joins the game in the other court.
4. Students must walk only on the lines of their court. If students step off the line to avoid being tagged, they must move to the other court.
5. Students can't pass each other on a line. If two students meet face to face, they must agree to travel in the same direction.
6. End the activity after 10 minutes.

> ⚠ SAFETY TIP
>
> Students should use gentle touches when tagging.

Eurofoam Mania

OBJECTIVES

Teamwork, communication, passing, throwing, cardiorespiratory endurance

EQUIPMENT

6 hula hoops, 6 basketball rims, 2 Eurofoam balls

SETUP

This activity requires three basketball courts. Hang the hula hoops over the basketball rims so that the hoops hang down partially below the backboard. The vertical hoops represent the goal area.

DIRECTIONS

1. Create six teams of equal size. Assign two teams per court, each with a Eurofoam ball.
2. Play begins with a throw-off, where one member of a team initiates play by throwing the ball to a teammate.
3. The opposing team tries to score a goal by throwing the ball through the opponent's hula hoop. Players may pass, slap, or kick the ball in any direction. Students in possession of the ball may run sideways or backward, but may not run forward while holding the ball. The rule of threes applies to getting rid of the ball and defending a player:
   - All players, offensive and defensive, must stay at least 3 feet (1 meter) away from the person with the ball.
   - Players must release the ball after 3 seconds of taking possession.
   - Three teammates must have possession of the ball before a score is attempted.
4. After a goal has been scored, play begins again with a throw-off by the defensive team.

Spin Tag

OBJECTIVES

Cardiorespiratory fitness, quickness, agility, personal-best challenge

EQUIPMENT

None

SETUP

This activity requires a well-defined space approximately the size of two basketball courts. Generally, the greater the space available, the less intense the activity is.

DIRECTIONS

1. Students try to tag as many players as they can in a designated amount of time. If tagged in the process, they have to spin around two times before they continue tagging.
2. Students count how many people they can tag in the amount of time provided, trying for a personal best in 30 seconds.
3. After three whistles, students take a knee and take their target heart rate (counting for 6 seconds and then adding a 0).
4. Repeat.
5. Extend the time to 45 seconds. Repeat.

Chicken–Tire Tag

OBJECTIVES

Cardiorespiratory endurance, dodging, fleeing, agility

EQUIPMENT

4-6 rubber chickens, 25 bicycle inner tubes (1 per pair of students), music player

SETUP

This activity requires a well-defined area.

DIRECTIONS

1. Divide the class into pairs. Each pair places an inner tube around them.
2. Select 4 to 6 pairs of students to be It and give each pair a rubber chicken.
3. At the signal, students who are It try to tag the other pairs using the beak of the rubber chicken. Once a pair is tagged, they are given the chicken and are now It.
4. After 5 to 10 minutes, provide a short rest and then play again.

> ⚠ SAFETY TIP
>
> The chicken is a tagging device, not a striking device. The chicken serves as an extension of the tagger's arm. Instruct students to gently use the beak of the chicken for tagging.

Pop or Be Popped

OBJECTIVES

Cardiorespiratory endurance, agility, dodging, fleeing

EQUIPMENT

1 balloon per student (plus extras), 1 12-inch (30-centimeter) piece of string per student

SETUP

This activity requires a well-defined indoor space; generally a basketball court is adequate for 40 to 50 students. As the group gets smaller, make the playing area smaller.

DIRECTIONS

1. Provide each student with a balloon and string. Students blow up their balloons and tie on their piece of string. Provide extras for students who accidently pop their balloon while setting up for the activity.
2. Space students evenly throughout the playing area.
3. On your signal, students run around, dragging their balloons on the floor behind them and attempting to pop other students' balloons by stomping on them. Students continue to play even if their balloons are popped.
4. Stop the activity when fewer than five students still have balloons.

VARIATIONS

- Shoe Poppers (level 1): Instead of holding the string, students tie it to their shoe.
- Partner Poppers (level 2): Use panty hose to tie two students together at the ankle. Each team has a balloon tied to one teammate's ankle. With their free foot, students attempt to pop other teams' balloons. Students continue to play even if their team balloon is popped.
- Dribble Poppers (level 3): Each student has a basketball and must dribble while playing. Emphasize proper dribbling skills. Players cannot throw their ball at their opponents' balloons to pop them. After a balloon is popped, that player either can go to an available basket to work on shooting skills or continue to play. This is a great way to develop dribbling skills since it forces students to keep their head up while playing.
- Balloon Rewards: A nice way to close this activity is to stop the game with four or fewer students left with their balloon. Sign the balloons with a happy face, "Have a great day," or some special saying and return the balloons to the students. They will then have a balloon to take with them for the day.

Balance Tag

OBJECTIVES

Spatial awareness, agility, dodging, fleeing

EQUIPMENT

1 beanbag per student, music player

SETUP

This activity requires a well-defined area.

DIRECTIONS

1. Divide the group into partners and give each student a beanbag. One of the partners is designated as the tagger, the other as the runner.
2. Students spread out throughout the playing area and put the beanbag on their head.
3. When the music starts, the taggers try to tag their partners, all while balancing the beanbags on their heads. If the beanbag falls off, students just pick it up, replace it on their head, and keep playing.
4. When the runner is tagged, partners switch roles.

> ⚠ SAFETY TIP
>
> Students should use gentle touches when tagging.

Trio Tag

EQUIPMENT

1 rubber chicken for every 4 students

SETUP

This activity requires a space the size of two basketball courts.

DIRECTIONS

1. Place the class into groups of four. In each group, designate three students as taggers and one student as the runner.
2. The taggers must carry the rubber chicken with them at all times, passing it back and forth as they chase the runner. They can't throw the chicken at the runner, but must tag the runner with it instead.
3. The tagger currently holding the chicken can't move and can only tag the runner or throw the chicken to a fellow tagger. The taggers must communicate and make fast, accurate passes while they try to surround the runner. They can also make fake moves to redirect the runner.

> ⚠ **SAFETY TIP**
>
> Students should use gentle touches when tagging.

TEACHING TIP

The group determines who will be tagged. Make sure students rotate so that all have the opportunity to be on the trio and to be tagged.

Smokers Tag

OBJECTIVES

Cardiorespiratory endurance, dodging, fleeing, agility

EQUIPMENT

2 or 3 foam noodles

SETUP

This activity requires a well-defined area.

DIRECTIONS

1. Select 2 or 3 students to be taggers and hand each one a noodle. All students spread out in the playing area.
2. Taggers try to tag as many runners as they can by touching them gently with a noodle.
3. When students are tagged, they must remain in place and cough until other students free them by performing five jumping jacks with them. While they are doing jumping jacks, they are safe from taggers.
4. The game is continuous and ends with your signal after 10 to 15 minutes.

> ⚠ **SAFETY TIP**
>
> Students should use gentle touches when tagging.

TEACHING TIP

Ask the following questions as teaching points on the dangers of smoking.

- What happened to players when they were tagged (the "smokers")? (They could no longer play, had to stop, and so on.)
- What saved the player? (Other players supported them by exercising with them. Discuss with students how they can support others to make good choices that promote health and wellness. For example, instead of smoking, students could suggest their friends do something fun like skateboarding, playing basketball, or swimming to avoid situations where they may be pressured or tempted to smoke.)

Teeter-Totter Tag

OBJECTIVES

Dodging, fleeing

EQUIPMENT

None

SETUP

This activity requires a well-defined playing area.

DIRECTIONS

1. Place students in groups of three. Each group plays Rock, Paper, Scissors (see page 21 in chapter 1) to determine which two students will join together to tag the third.
   - If all three show the same sign, they give each other high fives and play again.
   - If all three show different signs, they give each other low fives and play again.
   - When two students have the same sign and the third student has a different sign, continue to step 2.
2. The third student begins running immediately. Meanwhile, the other two students complete a teeter-totter. To do this, they face each other and join hands. The first student squats while the second remains standing, and then the second student squats while the first remains standing.
3. Once the pair has completed the teeter-totter, they link elbows and attempt to tag the runner.
4. Once tagged, the three resume Rock, Paper, Scissors and the game begins anew.

> ⚠ **SAFETY TIP**
>
> Students should use gentle touches when tagging.

Pass the Fat Tag

OBJECTIVES

Cardiorespiratory endurance, dodging, fleeing, agility

EQUIPMENT

4 or more painter sponges, 25 pairs of panty hose or bicycle inner tubes

SETUP

This activity requires a well-defined playing area.

DIRECTIONS

1. Divide the class into partners. Partners are connected with the panty hose or bicycle inner tube or are linked elbow in elbow.
2. Designate four or more pairs as It and give each pair a sponge.
3. Students who are tagged by the fat (sponge) freeze and count to five. The tagging team hands over the sponge and the tagged team becomes It.

> ### ⚠ SAFETY TIP
>
> Students should use gentle touches when tagging.

TEACHING TIP

Use this opportunity to talk about the problems of eating foods that are high in fat. Here are some teaching points:

- Once food has been consumed, the body must absorb the fat contained within the food.
- Sometimes friends encourage us to eat food high in fat. What can we do to avoid these situations?
- How difficult is it to rid our body of fat?

Mosquito Tag

OBJECTIVES

Cardiorespiratory endurance, agility, dodging, fleeing, teamwork

EQUIPMENT

At least 4 foam noodles

SETUP

This activity requires a well-defined area approximately the size of a basketball court.

DIRECTIONS

1. Place students in pairs, linked by holding hands or linking elbows.
2. Designate four or more pairs as mosquitoes and give each pair a noodle. They attempt to tag other pairs gently with the noodle.
3. When tagged, a pair must kneel until freed by another pair of students who give them high fives and yell out "Raid!" (the name of an insecticide).
4. Four pairs can kill a mosquito by joining together to form a line. The pairs must link by touching each other in any manner, such as standing shoulder to shoulder or holding hands. If the lead pair makes eye contact with a mosquito, they point at

the mosquito while all yell "Raid!" The students who were the mosquito drop their noodle, and the lead pair picks up the noodle and becomes the new mosquito.

5. Play continues until you stop the action, after 10 to 15 minutes.

> ⚠ **SAFETY TIP**
>
> Students should use gentle touches when tagging.

Knights Unite

OBJECTIVES

Teamwork, implementation of offensive and defensive strategies, communication

EQUIPMENT

1 hula hoop, 1 cone, and 1 foam ball per offensive team, plus an extra set

SETUP

Spread the hula hoops around an area the length of approximately two basketball courts; there should be one more hoop than there are offensive teams (so that no teams wait for an available hoop to play). Place a cone in the center of each hoop.

Introduce the game with this scenario: Long, long ago, there were two knights whose actions determined the fate of the world. The knights knew that teamwork could overcome great obstacles and trials. Their mission was to toss a ball of fire through the rings of eternity, but the task was not easy. Beasts guarded the rings and used all their skills to stop the knights from completing their task. And the mission did not stop when the ball was successfully tossed—there were many rings and many beasts. The knights could not get discouraged or tire, because their mission was to attack as many rings as they could each day.

DIRECTIONS

1. Divide the class into pairs. Designate half the class as offensive players (knights) and the other half plus two extra players as defensive players (beasts). The beasts are assigned to guard a specific hula hoop.

2. Each pair of knights receives one ball and goes to a hoop. The knights try to score by throwing their ball through the hoop. To do this, one of the knights grabs the hoop and tries to move it into position so that the other can throw the ball through it. The goaltending knight must keep one foot on the center cone at all times. The other knight must stay at least 3 feet (1 meter) away from the hoop while trying to find the best angle for throwing.

3. The two beasts guard the hoop and try to block the ball from going through. They can't touch either of the knights, but they can hit or catch the ball once it has been thrown. If the beasts catch the ball, they return it to the knights.

4. The knights stay at the hoop until they are successful. When the ball goes through, the knights earn 1 point, take their ball, and move on to a different available hoop.

5. Knights try to complete as many hoops as possible. The defending beasts stay with their hoop and wait for the next team of knights to approach.

6. Halfway through the class, take note of how many points the knights earned and then switch offensive and defensive players.

Beehives

OBJECTIVES

Dodging, fleeing

EQUIPMENT

6 foam noodles, 24 cones

SETUP

This game requires two adjacent playing areas (court A and court B), each approximately the size of a basketball court. The entrance to court A is located opposite that of court B. Divide each court into three even sections (hives) using cones to mark the boundaries. You can also play this game on grass, but make sure boundaries are well defined with cones.

DIRECTIONS

1. Designate six students as bees and give them a noodle and a hive to protect.
2. The rest of the students are bears. Half begin the game on court A, the other half on court B.
3. When the game starts, all bears run down the length of their court, running through the three hives while the bees try to sting them by tagging them with a noodle. For each hive they pass through without being stung, they earn 1 point.
4. Once they've completed a run without being stung, the bears jog along the outer sideline of their court back to the entrance of their hives.
5. If bears are stung within any of the hives, they complete the run to the end of their court but instead of jogging back to the entrance of their hive, they move next door to the other court's entrance and begin going through the hives of the other court.
6. Play is continuous. Bears count how many hives they are able to pass through without being stung.

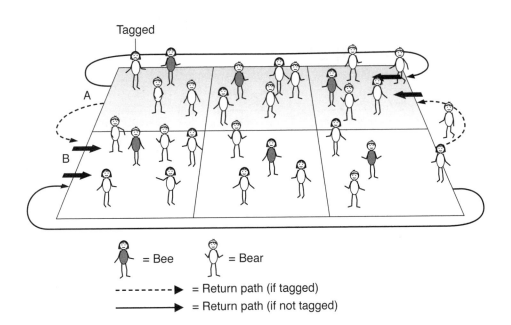

Two-Ball Challenge

OBJECTIVE

Teamwork

EQUIPMENT

6 crates, 100-200 tennis balls, 25 Z-Balls

SETUP

Disperse the balls throughout a bounded area approximately the size of a basketball court. Each team has three crates placed on the court. Increase distance to increase difficulty.

DIRECTIONS

1. Divide the class into two teams. Each team assigns a teammate to kick balls within the boundary for teammates to toss into crates.
2. Teams must stay outside the boundary lines.
3. When the game begins, kickers kick as many balls to their teammates as possible, who toss the balls into their team's crates.
4. Once a ball is in a crate, it is safe and cannot be removed.
5. Tennis balls are worth 1 point and Z-Balls are worth 5 points.
6. Play continues until all balls are in a crate or after 1 minute.

TEACHING TIPS

- This activity works best when it only lasts for 1 minute. This maximizes movement time, keeping all students active as they try to retrieve and toss balls.
- Multiple games can be played within a class; change kickers after each session.

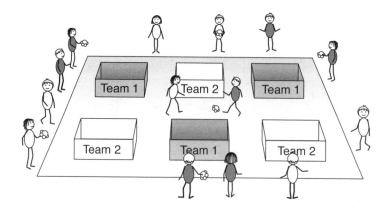

Ultimate Hockey or Soccer

OBJECTIVE

Cardiorespiratory fitness

EQUIPMENT

12 goals, 30 soft foam balls, foam noodles for half the class (for hockey), pinnies or wristbands for half the class

SETUP

This activity can be played as hockey with noodles or foam polo sticks, or as soccer by simply kicking the balls. Set up 12 goals around the edge of an area the size of a basketball court. Place 30 balls in the center of the area.

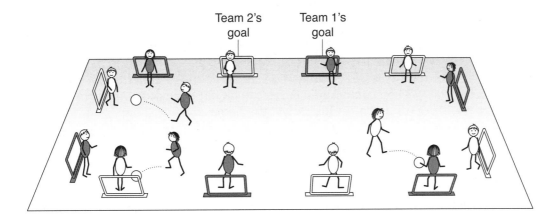

DIRECTIONS

1. Divide the class into two teams. Identify one team using pinnies or wristbands.
2. The teams provide one goalie to stand by each of their goals. The remaining students are kickers and stay in the center of the playing area.
3. Kickers must strike the ball with their foot (if playing soccer) or with a noodle (if playing hockey) into one of the other team's goals. When students make a goal, they run to you and give you a high five.
4. Whether the balls make a goal or not, the goalies toss them to their teammates in the middle of the room.
5. Continue play for the entire class, or for 20 to 30 minutes. Teams switch goalies on your signal.

TEACHING TIP

Students love to participate in this fast-paced game with many opportunities to score, make contact with the ball, and have fun. Ultimately, the score does not matter!

VARIATION

Teams can change their goalies at any time.

Cat and Mouse

OBJECTIVES

Dodging, fleeing

EQUIPMENT

None

SETUP

This activity requires an area approximately the size of a basketball half-court.

DIRECTIONS

1. Have the class form a circle by standing an arm's length apart from each other.
2. Choose one cat and one mouse from the class. The cat and mouse are positioned on opposite sides of the circle.
3. On your signal, the cat tries to tag the mouse. They can run around the circle or through the circle by passing between two students.
4. Once a cat or mouse passes between two students, those students join hands and the passageway becomes blocked. Neither the cat nor the mouse can move between those two students again for the rest of the game.
5. The game ends when the cat tags the mouse or when the entire circle becomes closed. Choose a new cat and a new mouse, and play again.

VARIATIONS

- Select two pairs of cats and mice. The cats can only chase their assigned mouse.
- Have the circle move slowly to the left or the right.

Monarchy Versus Anarchy

OBJECTIVES

Cardiorespiratory endurance, teamwork, cooperation

EQUIPMENT

3 foam or fleece balls

SETUP

This activity requires a fairly large area with boundaries.

DIRECTIONS

1. Select three pairs of students, and give each pair a ball. These students are members of the monarchy. All other students are anarchists.
2. Each pair of monarchs tries to tag an anarchist by throwing the ball. The monarch holding the ball can't move and can only pass the ball to the partner or throw it

at an anarchist. The monarchs must use teamwork to move the ball effectively and tag anarchists.

3. Anarchists dodge and flee to remain free. Any anarchists struck by a ball become members of the monarchy and join the students who tagged them.

4. The game continues until all anarchists have joined the monarchy.

TEACHING TIP

A group is most effective when everyone cooperates and works in a way that maximizes each individual effort. Ask students the following questions:

- What strategies worked best for you?
- What did you learn as an anarchist?
- How would the game be different if the monarchs did not work together?

Krazy Kones

OBJECTIVE

Cardiorespiratory endurance

EQUIPMENT

40 large cones, paper or dry-erase board for scoring

SETUP

In a defined playing area the size of a basketball court, randomly set up 40 cones.

DIRECTIONS

1. Divide students into two teams.

2. The game consists of four quarters, each lasting 60 to 90 seconds. During each quarter, the offensive team tries to knock down as many cones as possible, while the defending team tries to right as many cones as possible.

3. Students must follow these rules:
   - Offensive team members can't knock down the same cone twice in a row.
   - Offensive team members can knock down cones only with their hands.
   - Defenders must keep moving and can't stand by a cone to guard it.

4. At the end of the quarter, students take a knee while you count the number of cones knocked down. The number is the offensive team's knockdown score.

5. The teams play three more quarters, switching offensive and defensive roles each time.

6. After four quarters, the team with the highest total knockdown score is the winner.

TEACHING TIP

Ask students the following questions:

- What type of strategies did you use?
- Did you establish a zone or a stalker strategy (one-on-one coverage)?
- Was your response random? Or did you have a strategy on how to take down or set up?

VARIATION

Use pedometers to monitor workload. Ask students to reach a goal, such as 2,000 steps.

Fitness Scrabble

OBJECTIVES

Cardiorespiratory endurance, teamwork

EQUIPMENT

Index cards (the number of cards will be determined by the puzzle)

SETUP

This activity requires a playing area the width of a basketball court. Print the Barnyard Scrabble or Boneyard Scrabble handouts from the CD-ROM. (See reproducibles 2.10, "Barnyard Scrabble," and 2.11, "Boneyard Scrabble," on the CD-ROM.) On each card, write one letter needed to complete a word on the chosen handout. Place the cards facedown in a pile at one side of the playing area.

DIRECTIONS

1. Place students in groups of 4 or 5. Give each group one copy of the handout.
2. Groups send one member at a time to retrieve letters from the pile of cards at the other side of the playing area.
3. Runners must retrieve the first card they touch. They are not allowed to look through the stack to select a card.
4. They return with one card and see if it's a letter they need to complete a word on their handout. If so, they cross off that letter in a word on the handout.
5. The next runner returns the letter to the stack if it can't be used.

VARIATION

Students can create their own words derived from a theme, such as heart health, fitness terms, team sports, and so on.

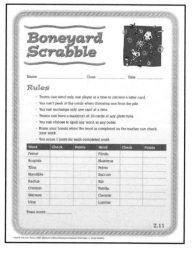

My Last Breath

OBJECTIVE

Understanding principles of cardiorespiratory health

EQUIPMENT

4 cones; pins or clips to attach doctor badges; 1 doctor badge per student; 1 straw per student; 1 Aerobic Institute Medical Chart per student; 1 My Last Breath worksheet per pair; 1 pencil per pair

SETUP

Evenly space the cones around a track or well-defined loop that the students can run along. Print My Last Breath worksheets (1 per pair of students), Aerobic Institute Medical Chart worksheets (1 per student), and doctor badges (1 per student) from the CD-ROM.

DIRECTIONS

1. Divide the class into pairs. In each pair, designate one student as the patient and the other as the doctor. Give each pair one My Last Breath worksheet, two Aerobic Institute Medical Charts, and two doctor badges. (See reproducibles 2.12, "My Last Breath," 2.13, "Aerobic Institute Medical Chart," and 2.14, "Doctor Badges," on the CD-ROM.)

2. The patient runs around the track while the doctor records how many cones the patient passes in 2 minutes. If the time is up while the patient is in between cones, the doctor counts the next cone not yet reached.

3. The students pretend that it's now 20 years later, and the patients have returned for another checkup after smoking heavily since the last visit. This time, the patients place a straw in their mouth and perform the 2-minute run while breathing only through the straw. The patients can't remove the straw from their mouth during the 2 minutes. If they do, the time ends and they receive the score they completed at the time they removed the straw.

4. Students switch roles and start again.

TEACHING TIP

How did you feel running with the straw? Smoking damages the lungs, leaving people gasping for breath, like breathing through a straw.

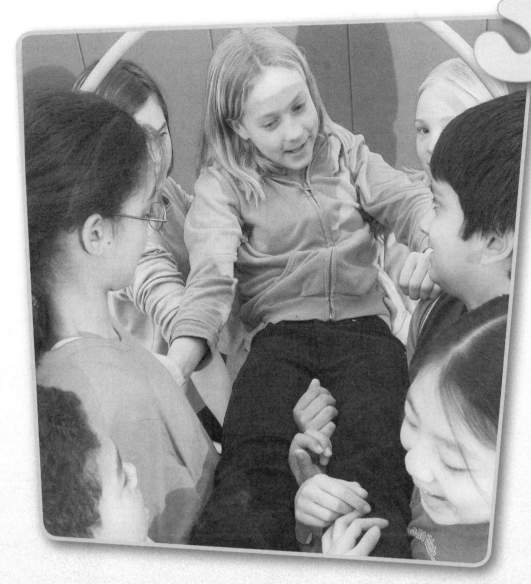

Social Skills Development

> **"O**ne of the secrets of life is to make stepping stones out of stumbling blocks."
>
> —*Jack Penn*

Social skills are more important than ever in today's schools, which include students from across the globe who speak different languages and come from different backgrounds. As we learn more about interconnecting systems, we begin to realize how our daily decisions influence the course of our lives and the lives of our students, not to mention our community and our world. As human beings, we are responsible for our actions and how they affect others, which means that helping students develop social skills is crucial. MOOMBA is the attitude we strive to develop in our children. As they learn and practice the skills to thrive, they learn how to develop relationships that reflect positive living.

Physical education provides a unique opportunity to help children develop such skills. Winning a game, an event, or a challenge brings out students' true character. No other curriculum reveals children's personal value systems through play. Physical educators should take advantage of the unique benefits of physical education to teach leadership skills, conflict resolution, cooperation, communication skills, respect, responsibility, trustworthiness, perseverance, kindness, and compassion.

This chapter includes themes and initiatives that highlight social skills. Group initiatives provide a lab setting that is explicit in its purpose: to develop social skills. They're a great way to allow students to experience these skills in a controlled setting.

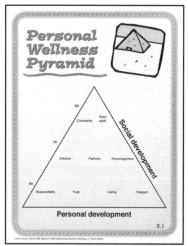

The Personal Wellness Pyramid represents the building blocks of desirable character traits embedded within the physical education curriculum. (See reproducible 3.1, "Personal Wellness Pyramid," on the CD-ROM.) Social skills are developed through purposeful, sequential learning experiences that build on previous lessons. For instance, sixth graders learn respect, responsibility, caring, and trust before they fully assume the responsibilities of citizenship and fairness. These traits build on one another and are reinforced throughout the year. The lessons must be explicit, and debriefing the activity is essential. Students need to understand why it's important to be respectful and practice those skills.

Elements of a Successful Social Skills Curriculum

For students to internalize an experience, they need to think about how their behaviors reflect their personal values. This requires teachers to explain the purpose of group initiatives by using debriefing techniques and helping students define how they will treat others. First, the work must be viewed by students as so important that they arrive at class with the specific expectation that they will reflect on their behavior, their attitude, and their value system and how they affect others. As a teacher, you model the skills you expect students to use. Recognize students for their positive choices, and look for behaviors that reflect those values through ongoing assessments.

Second, parents must see concrete examples of what is being taught and how they can support the lessons. Student values are indicative of parent values; therefore, group initiatives provide an opportunity for parents to reflect with their children on tolerance, respect, and responsibility. Third, parents must understand the value of physical education. Physical education is not only a place to learn how to be physically fit, but it's also a place to learn how to develop healthy habits for life—physical, social, and emotional. As parents become partners in our work, they begin to understand the important role physical education plays in the development of their child.

Promoting Social Skills

Post important social skills and your expectations for students. (See reproducibles 3.2, "Social Skill Cards," and 3.3, "Stars Recognition Award," on the CD-ROM.) Most importantly,

model the behavior and celebrate positive student behaviors that reflect those expectations.

Debriefing

Debriefing is a skill that is developed through time and experience. Be patient and continue to perfect your skill. Students need opportunities to understand how to change their behavior and make the world a better place for themselves and others. It's vital to take the time to debrief each group initiative by having students think about what skills they were developing during the activity. Group initiatives alone will not develop skills; you develop the skills by establishing clear expectations for student behavior, teaching the skills, and reinforcing behaviors that reflect the skills.

Discuss with students the characteristics of skills that they are expected to develop. What does the skill look like, sound like, and feel like? Students must see it, do it, and practice it. For example, in the Bull-Ring Transport activity, students learn how to encourage each other. Throughout the activity, you could ask the students the following questions:

- What would you like to see a classmate do to encourage you to take risks?
- What would you like to hear a classmate say to you to encourage you?

Students should practice encouraging actions, such as making eye contact, communicating solutions in a positive tone, bending their knees to be prepared to assist others, and so on. As they begin using words that support others, such as, "You can do it," "I'm here for you," and "That's the way to do it," they begin to feel what it's like to be encouraging. This helps them become aware of how their behavior affects others. Do they support others? Do others feel safe around them? How can they be a more positive member of the team? These are questions students should ask themselves, and they should be open to how others perceive them.

Here are some general debriefing questions to use at the conclusion of activities.

- How effective were we in accomplishing our goal?
- What could we have done differently?
- What role did you play in your team? Was your behavior helping or hindering the outcome?
- What will you do differently to get a better result?

When debriefing an activity, it's important to establish rules for student discussion. Such rules might include the following:

- One person speaks at a time. (You may want to create a talking piece, such as a tennis ball, bandanna, or other readily available object, so students learn to respect other speakers.)
- Use active listening when others speak (see chapter 1).
- Respect all comments.
- Resolve differences in a respectful manner.

It can be more powerful if students create their own rules. Post the rules and remind students of them when beginning a debriefing.

Facilitating

As a facilitator or as you train students to facilitate their own discussions, remember to guide them toward closure. Have a clear objective on what you want students to take away from the discussion by

- keeping students focused on the question,
- having students build on others' ideas,
- keeping students on the topic, and
- having students use examples from the activity to illustrate their point.

Developing the Curriculum

A good strategy is to spend the first 2 weeks of the school year in group initiatives to establish class norms, develop a sense of community, and reinforce social skills such as respect, responsibility, inclusiveness, cooperation, and kindness. Expect students to walk the walk through their words and deeds—and be sure to model those behaviors yourself during class time. Expect students to treat one another with respect, kindness, and fairness. Teach them active listening skills and practice those skills every day for the first 2 weeks. Hold students accountable for their learning by giving them an active listening quiz. In addition, incorporate a group initiative at least once per week throughout the year to reinforce and build on previous learning. An active listening quiz given to students informs them how important it is to listen. Use the Active Listening worksheet to assess what they know. (See reproducible 3.4 on the CD-ROM.)

Sample Schedules

The purpose of developing a schedule is to allow you to coordinate activities to build on one another. Following are sample schedules used for grades 6 through 8:

- The sixth grade schedule (figure 3.1) focuses on identifying strengths and weaknesses in communication skills, cooperation, respect, and leadership. ("Who am I?")
- The seventh grade schedule (figure 3.2) focuses on teamwork. ("How effective am I as a team member?")
- The eighth grade schedule (figure 3.3) focuses on problem-solving skills and more complex tasks with a greater degree of challenge.

Week	Location	Day	Activity
2	Multipurpose room	1	Hi, How Are You? Gotta Go Thumb Wrestling Random Acts of Kindness Three Hs
	Multipurpose room	2	Data Processing Compass Don't Touch Me
	Multipurpose room	3	Diminishing Circle

FIGURE 3.1 Sample sixth grade schedule for weeks 2 and 3.

Week	Location	Day	Activity
2 *(cont'd)*	Multipurpose room	4	Partner Get-Up Group Get-Up Affirmation Circle
	Multipurpose room	5	Mystical Wave Rock, Paper, Scissors Hog Call
3	Tennis court	6	Courtesy Tag Partner Pull Tricky Triangle
	Tennis court	7	Foot-Pass Train Beam Out
	Gym	8	Star Gate
	Gym	9	Form a Letter Random Acts of Kindness
	Gym	10	Knights Unite Traffic Jam

FIGURE 3.1 *(continued)* Sample sixth grade schedule for weeks 2 and 3.

Week	Day	Activity
Week 2	1	Hi, How Are You? Gotta Go Data Processing Thumb Wrestling
	2	Rock, Paper, Scissors Courtesy Tag Back to Back
	3	All Aboard Shark Bait
	4	Compass Don't Touch Me Diminishing Circle
	5	Random Count Finger Trap Group Get-Up
Week 3	6	Classroom Temperature Dowel Exchange Half-Tennis-Ball Elbow Snatch
	7	Neat Puzzle No-Rope Tug
	8	Pipeline
	9	River Crossing
	10	Bull-Ring Transport

FIGURE 3.2 Sample seventh grade schedule for weeks 2 and 3.

Week	Day	Activity
Week 2	1	Card Ranking
	2	Half the Feet Houdini Hoops
	3	Jurassic Planet Monarchy Versus Anarchy
	4	Partner Get-Up Pop or Be Popped Affirmation Circle
	5	Hula Hoop Relay Scrum Soccer
Week 3	6	Tanks and Commanders Speed Count
	7	Dome Balance
	8	Minefield
	9	Stock Market
	10	Boardroom

FIGURE 3.3 Sample eighth grade schedule for weeks 2 and 3.

Activities With a Purpose: Teaching Social Skills

The activities in this chapter are designed to prompt discussion about leadership, teamwork, and communication. Students will examine how they can become more effective in achieving a common goal through teamwork, communication, and leadership. The social skills curriculum in this chapter is just a small portion of activities that have been developed. Whatever activities you choose to incorporate, the key component is the time you spend debriefing the activity. Students gain insights through thoughtful reflection on their behavior and how it affected group performance. Debriefing is a great opportunity to teach students the connection between individual choices and their impact on others.

As discussed earlier, in order for students to learn social skills, they must experience them and practice them. The key is to consistently reinforce the skills in class and throughout the entire year.

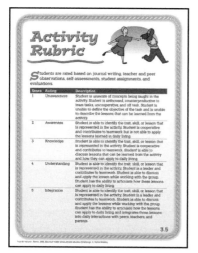

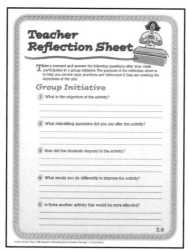

Using assessments helps students identify the specific skills targeted and also reflect on their behavior. Incorporate assessments into these activities to ensure students are learning to use the skills rather than just playing games. You should see more students using the skills desired for greater group performance, such as the following:

- Encouraging words
- Respect for others' perspectives
- Positive conflict resolution techniques:
  - Good listening
  - Presenting arguments that support outcomes
  - Willingness to try suggestions

The reproducibles included on the CD-ROM are designed to provide a structured approach to help students become introspective on how they interact with others. By creating time within the curriculum to reflect on student behavior, we are communicating to them that social skill development, leadership, teamwork, and everything involved in becoming a productive member of a group are priorities in physical education. Many times this standard within physical education is viewed as a by-product of a team or game setting; however, the skill is never overtly taught even though it may be a required need for many students. Use these sheets throughout the year, and revisit goals or behaviors to allow students to make conscientious choices to make positive changes. See reproducibles 3.5, "Activity Rubric," 3.6, "Teacher Reflection Sheet," 3.7, "Think About It (Student Reflection Sheet)," 3.8, "Weekly Traits (Student Reflection Sheet)," and 3.9, "Look in the Mirror (Group Evaluation)," on the CD-ROM.

Toe Tag

OBJECTIVE

Team building

EQUIPMENT

1 fleece ball per student

SETUP

This activity requires a well-defined playing area the size of a tennis court.

DIRECTIONS

1. Divide students into pairs and give each student a fleece ball.
2. Demonstrate how students will maintain contact with each other during the activity. One student places his left hand on the right shoulder of his partner, while the other places his right hand on the left shoulder of his partner.
3. While staying connected, students take turns tossing their fleece ball at the foot of their partner, trying to hit one foot. They earn 1 point for every strike. Students must fake and have quick feet to avoid being tagged.

VARIATIONS

- Students see how many contacts they can make in 30 seconds.
- Students throw using the right hand and then the left hand.

Data Processing

OBJECTIVES

Getting to know other students, team building

EQUIPMENT

None

SETUP

This activity requires an area the size of a basketball half-court. Before class, come up with multiple ways for sorting students in a lineup, such as by eye color, hair color, hair length, height, age, birth date, birth month, number of teeth missing or remaining, and so on. Be creative!

DIRECTIONS

1. Ask students to line up according to a specific criterion (see Setup for ideas).
2. Allow students to problem solve how to organize themselves to meet the criteria determined by you.
3. Once students are lined up, review the line and determine whether they accurately followed the criterion.

TEACHING TIP

It's important to allow as much freedom as necessary for students to communicate and problem solve the activity.

VARIATIONS

- Add a time limit for students to complete a lineup.
- Require students to successfully complete the lineup without talking.

Don't Touch Me

OBJECTIVES

Respecting personal space of others, self-awareness

EQUIPMENT

None

SETUP

The playing area should be the size of a tennis half-court or smaller.

DIRECTIONS

1. Place students around the perimeter of the playing area.
2. Instruct students to cross to the opposite side of the playing area without touching anyone while they cross. If anyone is touched, stop the activity to briefly ask students what they could do differently, and then start the activity again.

TEACHING TIPS

- This activity is a great lead-up to a tag game and trains students how to move from place to place while being aware and respectful of others.
- When you place a time limit on the activity or put a hula hoop in the center of the playing area, students will need to problem solve and communicate in order to be successful.

VARIATIONS

- Add a hula hoop in the middle of the playing area. Students must place at least one foot in the center of the hula hoop before going to the other side.
- Time the activity to see how fast the group can complete the task.

Compass

OBJECTIVES

Problem-solving skills, communication skills

EQUIPMENT

None

SETUP

This activity requires an area approximately the size of a basketball half-court.

DIRECTIONS

1. Instruct students to form a square with an equal number of students on each side.
2. You are in the center of the square and ask students to remember their position in the square and in relationship to you. They must remember if they are facing your back, front, right side, or left side.
3. After you count to three, change positions. Students must regroup so they are in the same position in relation to you. For example, if you are facing the south side of the square and then turn to face the west side, all students must move so they are in the same placement and relationship to you.
4. Face another side of the square, stand there, and count to three.
5. Students again move from their spots and place themselves in their original position.

TEACHING TIPS

- Some students are very good at spatial relationships, but are others willing to listen to them? This is a good problem-solving activity that takes some practice for students to master.
- Students will perform better if they remember who was on their right and left as well as their relationship to you when the activity began.

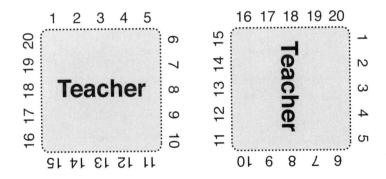

Tanks and Commanders

OBJECTIVES

Communication skills, cooperation

EQUIPMENT

1 blindfold per pair of students, 50 fleece balls

SETUP

Scatter the fleece balls within a well-defined area approximately the size of a tennis half-court.

DIRECTIONS

1. Divide the class into pairs. Pairs decide who is going to be the tank and who is going to be the commander. The tank puts on a blindfold.
2. The commander provides verbal cues for the tank to find a fleece ball.
3. Once the tank is loaded (has a fleece ball), the commander provides verbal instructions on the location of another tank.
4. When directed to fire by the commander, the tank must toss (not throw) the fleece ball with her nondominant hand at another tank.
5. If the tank is hit, he changes roles with his commander. Commanders may protect their tanks from being hit by knocking down any incoming balls, but they can never touch their tanks.
6. Activity is continuous for 8 to 12 minutes.

Triangle Tag

OBJECTIVES

Cooperation, appropriate play

EQUIPMENT

None

SETUP

This activity requires an area approximately the size of a basketball half-court.

DIRECTIONS

1. Place students in groups of four.
2. Designate one student as It. The other three face each other and join hands, forming a triangle.
3. Select one student in the triangle as the target.

4. The student who is It tries to tag the target student. The three students must work together to protect the target from being tagged. The person who is It can run freely and reach under arms or around to reach the target.

5. Once the target has been tagged, students change roles so that the target is It and another student becomes the new target. Players rotate so that everyone has an opportunity to be the target and It.

Star Gate

OBJECTIVES

Teamwork, cooperation

EQUIPMENT

50 hula hoops or bicycle inner tubes, 5 bandannas for every 6 students

SETUP

Scatter the hula hoops around an area the size of a tennis court. Place them at varying distances from each other, from touching each other to no more than 2 feet (61 centimeters) apart.

DIRECTIONS

1. Divide the class into groups of six and have them line up side by side.

2. Using bandannas, tie the ankles of students with those of the people next to them.

3. Students try to safely maneuver their group from one side of the playing area to the other through the star gates (hula hoops).

4. Students can only step within hula hoops. They must plan, communicate, and support each other in order to move from hoop to hoop since no single hoop can hold all six players.

Walk-a-Hula

OBJECTIVES

Teamwork, communication

EQUIPMENT

4 hula hoops for every 6 students

SETUP

This activity requires an area approximately the size of a basketball half-court.

DIRECTIONS

1. Place students in groups of six and provide each group with four hula hoops.

2. Instruct students to place three students side by side, shoulder to shoulder. Students face the same direction.

3. Place the remaining three students directly behind the first set of students, facing the same direction.

4. The center students place their right leg in one hula hoop and their left leg in the other.

5. The students to the right place their left leg in the hula hoop and the students on the left place their right leg in the hula hoop.

6. Students raise the hula hoops to their knees and apply pressure to keep them in place.

7. Without using their hands to hold up the hula hoops, the students must walk the width of the basketball court.

TEACHING TIP

Follow up with Hula Hoop Lava Crossing and Fire Escape (Hula Hoop Lava Crossing is a variation of River Crossing on page 89; see page 98 for Fire Escape). Combine two teams to form teams of 12.

Dutch Relay

OBJECTIVES

Teamwork, communication

EQUIPMENT

3-foot (1-meter) PVC pipe with a diameter of approximately 3 inches (8 centimeters) and 30-40 holes drilled in the sides for each group of 5 or 6 students, 2 garbage cans per group

SETUP

Fill half of the garbage cans with water and place the empty cans 25 yards (23 meters) from the filled cans. Mark a line on the inside of the empty trash cans; this is how full the teams must fill the cans with water.

DIRECTIONS

1. Group students into teams of 5 or 6 and place them behind the garbage can filled with water.

2. Provide each team with a PVC pipe. The teams' goal is to be the first to transport enough water from their garbage can to reach the line on their empty garbage can. They must transport their water only using the PVC pipe, working as a team to plug the holes while transporting and dumping the water into the empty trash can.

TEACHING TIPS

- Students will have to problem solve and discover how they must work together as a team to plug the holes to maximize the amount of water transported during each trip.
- Students get really wet trying to accomplish the task. You may wish to complete this activity on a Friday so students can take their gym clothes home that night.

River Crossing

OBJECTIVES

Teamwork, communication

EQUIPMENT

2 2- x 4- x 12-inch (5- x 10- x 30-centimeter) boards for each group of 6 students, 3 poly spots per group

SETUP

This activity requires an area approximately the size of a basketball court.

DIRECTIONS

1. Place students into teams of six and provide them with two boards and three poly spots.
2. Students must cross the river (basketball court) with their islands (boards and poly spots).
3. Students may not step in the river or touch the river with any other body part.
4. All students must cross the river together. A team of three cannot cross and send one student back with the equipment so that the remaining four members can cross.

TEACHING TIPS

- This is a great activity for asking debriefing questions to improve team communication, problem-solving skills, and conflict resolution. Students must be creative in moving the islands across the river.
- Increase the level of difficulty by removing a piece of equipment from teams whose members stepped in the river. Another option is to require students to wear a bandanna, or use only one leg or one arm, if they place a body part in the river.

VARIATION

Hula Hoop Lava Crossing: Instead of poly spots and boards, provide teams of 8 to 12 players with four hula hoops. Increase the distance to the width of a soccer field. This variation is best played outside but can also be played indoors. If students contact the ground outside of the hula hoop, the group must begin again. See how quickly a team can cross.

Traffic Jam

OBJECTIVES

Teamwork, communication skills, problem solving

EQUIPMENT

9 poly spots for every 8 students

SETUP

Place nine poly spots in a line in an area approximately the size of a tennis half-court. The four poly spots to either side of the center spot will be occupied by students facing the middle. Place enough sets of poly spots to accommodate the entire class.

DIRECTIONS

1. Divide the group into teams of eight. To begin, four students stand on the places to the left of the middle poly spot, and the other four stand to the right. Whether to the left or right, students face the center vacant poly spot.

2. Students on the left side must end up in the places on the right side, and vice versa, using the following guidelines.

   • Players may move into an empty space in front of them.
   • Players may move around others who are facing them into an empty space.
   • No one can move backward.
   • No one can step around someone who is facing the same way.
   • Only one person can move at a time.

3. When groups find the solution, have them show it to you.

TEACHING TIP

Remember, students cannot move backward and can only move to the space immediately in front of them or the space behind someone who is facing them. Here is the order of student moves: 4, 5, 6, 4, 3, 2, 5, 6, 7, 8, 4, 3, 2, 1, 5, 6, 7, 8, 3, 2, 1, 7, 8, 1.

Here is an example to illustrate how this works. In part a, 1 may move into the empty space because two people are facing one another. In part b, 1 can move around 2 into the empty space immediately behind because 2 is facing 1.

VARIATION

If you do not have exact groups of eight, teams can substitute a cone for a member of their team. Someone from the team is responsible for moving the cone as if it were a student.

Tricky Triangle

OBJECTIVES

Teamwork, problem-solving skills

EQUIPMENT

40-50 poly spots (or chalk to mark the spots)

SETUP

In an area approximately the size of a basketball court, create 4 or 5 triangles by placing 10 poly spots in the same formation as 10 pins in bowling.

DIRECTIONS

1. Divide the class into teams of 10.
2. Ask them to arrange themselves into standing 4-3-2-1 pyramids.
3. Once arranged, students must reverse the triangle 180 degrees by moving only three people.

Solution:

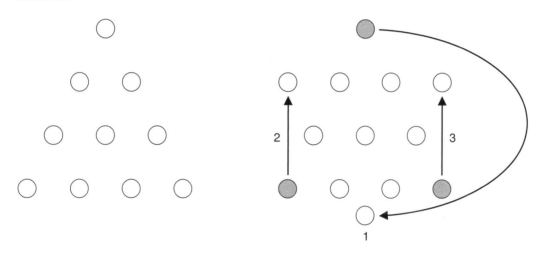

Shark Attack

OBJECTIVES

Communication, compassion, helpfulness

EQUIPMENT

1 parachute, 3 pinnies

SETUP

Lay a parachute flat in the center of the playing area.

DIRECTIONS

1. Select two students to be sharks and three students to be lifeguards. The lifeguards wear pinnies, which represent life vests. The rest of the students sit around the perimeter of the parachute with their legs extended.

2. Students hold the parachute with both hands and bring it up to their waist, elevating the parachute from the ground approximately 1 foot (30 centimeters).

3. The sharks go under the parachute and begin to swim while students create waves with the parachute (they can also shake the parachute to simulate turbulent water), and the lifeguards walk the perimeter of the parachute.

4. The sharks try to bring students under the parachute by grabbing their ankles and pulling. The victims yell for the lifeguards to help them. They are not allowed to kick or try to escape the grasp of the shark.

5. If a victim is saved (tagged) by a lifeguard before the shark can pull the victim under, the victim changes places with the lifeguard. The lifeguard, who is now a swimmer, can select a place anywhere around the parachute to enter the game.

6. If the shark is able to pull a student under the parachute before a lifeguard arrives, the entire class hums a sad song. The victim becomes a shark and play continues.

7. Play is called when there are five swimmers left. From the five, select two as sharks and three as lifeguards and resume play.

⚠ **SAFETY TIP**

Lifeguards and sharks should not play tug-of-war with the victim.

Beam-Out

OBJECTIVES

Teamwork, communication, problem-solving skills

EQUIPMENT

1 tarp with a 4- to 6-inch (10- to 15-centimeter) hole in the center for each group of 4-6 students, 10 tennis balls per group, 1 bucket per group

SETUP

Place one tennis ball per team at one end of an area approximately the size of a basketball court.

Tell students the following: They are scientists sent to investigate a new life form on planet Zobatar. Their mission is to successfully transport alien droppings discovered by the landing party. Because they must protect themselves from any unseen alien probes, they must use the beam-out blanket (tarp) and move the objects to the beaming station for a beam-out. No student is allowed to touch the droppings at any time; doing so may result in injury and possible death. If a student touches the ball, you determine the consequence. The severity of the consequence depends on the maturity and skill of the students. Students who touched the ball may have to place an arm behind their back, close their eyes, or hold the hand of another. If students continue to touch a ball, you may wish to send them "into orbit" (walk around the playing area before returning to the game). Students are never eliminated or removed from the game.

DIRECTIONS

1. Place students in groups of 4 to 6 and provide them with a beam-out blanket (tarp). Select one student to be the alien who places a tennis ball on the baseline for each team.

2. The teams stand at the baseline of the basketball court at the opposite end from the tennis balls.

3. On your signal, an alien will place a tennis ball on the opposite side from each team. Teams must go to the other end of the court and place their blanket over the ball so it goes through the hole onto the blanket. Everyone on a team must remain in contact with the beam-out blanket at all times.

4. Once the ball is on the blanket, students must manipulate the blanket to successfully carry the ball to their bucket. Then they manipulate the blanket to allow the ball to drop through the hole into the bucket. Teams must then return to get another tennis ball. Once all balls or alien droppings are transported to the bucket, the droppings can be beamed out by having the team make three rotations around the bucket, sit down, and yell "Zobatar!"

Scrum Soccer

OBJECTIVES

Cooperation, teamwork

EQUIPMENT

1 ball for each group of 5-7 students, 1 bucket per group, 15 cones

SETUP

Scatter the cones throughout an area approximately the size of a soccer field. Place the buckets at one end of the field.

DIRECTIONS

1. Divide the class into teams of 5 to 7. Teams group together into a tight circle, like a rugby scrum, at the end of the field that is opposite the buckets. Place a ball in the center of each scrum.

2. On your signal, students use their feet to move the ball to the other end of the field, circling the ball around every cone on the field. Teams can circle the cones in any order, but they may not use their hands or break the circle at any time.

3. Once students have circled all 15 cones, they are allowed to cross the opposite end zone and place the ball in their team bucket using their feet.

Boardroom

OBJECTIVES

Teamwork, communication, patience, critical thinking

EQUIPMENT

4 hula hoops, 16 2- × 8-inch (5- × 20-centimeter) boards at least 6 feet (2 meters) long

SETUP

In an area approximately the size of a basketball half-court, create four stations by placing a hula hoop in the center and arranging four planks around the hoop in a plus sign.

DIRECTIONS

1. Place students in groups of 12 to 20 and assign them to stations.
2. Team members each select a board to stand on. They must distribute themselves equally between the four boards at their station so that there are 3 to 5 students per board.
3. On your signal, students move from one board to another within their station, going through the hula hoop by placing both feet in the center before moving to another board. They must always be in contact with either a board or the platform (hula hoop) at all times. At the conclusion of movement, students must be on a different board with no member of their original board on their new board.

VARIATIONS

- Have students complete the challenge without touching each other.
- Students must end up in a position that is different than their original board position. For instance, if they began the activity last in line on their board, they must end up on another board with none of their original board members, standing in any position other than the last position in line.

Hula Hoop Relay

OBJECTIVES

Communication, passing, teamwork, sprinting

EQUIPMENT

1 hula hoop for every 6 students

SETUP

Line up the hula hoops behind the end zone of a soccer field.

DIRECTIONS

1. Place students in teams of six and have them line up single file in front of their hula hoop. Students can decide how far to space themselves from each other. The farther apart they spread their line, the fewer passes they have to make, but they also increase the risk of dropping a hoop.

2. The person closest to the hula hoop, player 1, picks up the hoop and passes it to the next person in line. Player 1 then runs to the front of the line.

3. Player 2 passes to player 3, player 3 to player 4, and so on until it reaches player 6, who then passes to player 1.

4. Teammates continue to pass the hula hoop until they reach the other end zone. The object of the activity is to see how quickly they can accomplish this.

5. If students drop the hula hoop, the team must return to the beginning and start again.

VARIATIONS

- Students see how quickly they can pass the hoop up the field and back two times. They yell "Hooray!" when done.

- Students see how many times they can move the hoop up the field and back in 1 minute.

- Designate a runner from each team who runs backward and tries to outrun the group while they pass the hula hoop up the field and back.

Minefield

OBJECTIVES

Communication, trust, active listening

EQUIPMENT

4-20 blindfolds, various objects (e.g., ropes, cones, rubber chickens, Frisbees, bowling pins, carpet squares)

SETUP

Scatter the objects around a defined area approximately the size of a tennis half-court.

DIRECTIONS

1. Place students in pairs. Designate one as the traveler and the other as the guide. The traveler must wear a blindfold.

2. The guide cannot enter the minefield (playing area) at any time but must use verbal directions to guide the traveler through the minefield to reach the other side safely.

3. If the traveler touches any of the objects or another traveler, the traveler must remove the blindfold, return to the starting line, and begin again.

4. After the traveler completes the task, the partners switch roles.

TEACHING TIPS

- Give examples of good directions provided by student guides. Why were they more helpful than other directions provided?
- Ask whether anyone was frustrated during this activity. If students say they were, ask why they were frustrated, how they handled the frustration, and whether they would do anything differently.
- Ask how students can use what they learned to better communicate with each other in class.

VARIATIONS

- Larger groups can break into teams rather than pairs. If using teams, either one person can try to guide all the others through the minefield or a group of people can try to guide a single traveler.
- In groups of three, blindfold two partners, who use scooter boards to navigate the minefield while a guide directs them from the sideline.
- Have travelers walk backward through the minefield blindfolded while their guides direct them from the sideline.

Neat Puzzle

OBJECTIVES

Teamwork, communication, patience, critical thinking

EQUIPMENT

Set of poly spots numbered 1-9 for each group of 8 students; timer or stopwatch; 9- × 9-foot (3- × 3-meter) grid subdivided into 3-foot (1-meter) squares (use chalk on the ground or use a tarp and permanent ink) for each group

SETUP

Create enough grids for teams of eight students. Arrange the sets of poly spots on the grids in random order with the numbers facedown.

DIRECTIONS

1. Form groups of eight and assign each member within the team a number from 1 through 8.
2. Students step into their team's grid and select one poly spot to stand on. Because there are eight students standing in a grid of nine spots, there will always be one vacant poly spot.
3. Students begin the activity by flipping over the vacant poly spot to discover its number.
4. Once a poly spot is flipped, it must be returned facedown. The team must remember its number and placement.
5. Students move one at a time so they end up on the poly spot that matches their assigned number. For example, if a student is a three, she moves so that she ends up on spot 3. In moving, students must follow certain rules:

- Only a vacant poly spot can be turned and read.
- Only one person can stand on a spot at a time.
- Students can only move linearly, not diagonally, from spot to spot.
- Students cannot make two consecutive moves.

6. Once the task is completed, reshuffle the poly spots and start again.

Protect Your Turf

OBJECTIVES

Teamwork, defense and offense, throwing for accuracy

EQUIPMENT

1 lightweight, 1-foot (30-centimeter) cone or empty tennis can and 1 tennis ball per student

SETUP

Place equal numbers of cones in each quadrant of a gym or tennis court.

DIRECTIONS

1. Have students choose a cone to stand by and then hand each person one tennis ball.
2. Students throw their ball to knock down the cone of a student from another quadrant. They are not allowed to knock down cones within their own quadrant. They also cannot leave their quadrant, but they can leave their cone unattended to retrieve a tennis ball. They are allowed to deflect balls to protect their cones.
3. Once a cone has been knocked down, the student is not allowed to set it back up but can continue to retrieve balls to throw or to help protect other members' cones within their quadrant.
4. The game ends when at least one cone is remaining or when you call an end to the game.

> ⚠ **SAFETY TIP**
>
> Students are not allowed to throw the ball at players or at eye level.

VARIATION

Divide the class into two teams, each with the same number of targets to protect. Each team can decide what strategy to use. For example, everyone can continue to play both offense and defense, or the team can designate specific players to perform specific tasks, such as offense, defense, or ball collection.

Fire Escape

OBJECTIVES

Teamwork, appropriate touch, communication, sharing space safely, trust

EQUIPMENT

6 hula hoops per group of 12-15 students, 4 cones

SETUP

Prepare the activity area by clearly marking a starting line using the cones.

DIRECTIONS

1. Place students in teams of 12 to 15 and provide each team with six hula hoops.
2. Instruct teams to place their hula hoops in a single, straight line in front of them. Students then line up behind the first hula hoop.
3. On your signal, one by one students step from hoop to hoop until they reach the last hula hoop.
4. The first student to arrive at the sixth hula hoop waits inside the hoop until each teammate arrives, being careful to take in all students one at a time. This requires the ability to gather in a tight space and keep all teammates safe while doing so.
5. When all students reach the sixth hula hoop, they stay there until you call out "Evacuation!" Students then run single file back to the starting point and the activity starts again.

TEACHING TIP

Try this activity right after Walk-a-Hula (page 87) or Hula Hoop Lava Crossing (page 89).

Speed Count

OBJECTIVES

Teamwork, communication, patience, critical thinking

EQUIPMENT

Chalk or 1 set of poly spots numbered 1-25 for each group of 13-15 students, timer or stopwatch

SETUP

Use chalk to create sufficient playing stations to accommodate groups of 13 to 15 students; each station is approximately 15 by 15 feet (4.5 by 4.5 meters). Within each square, randomly arrange a set of poly spots numbered 1 through 25, or use chalk to create 25 circles numbered 1 through 25 in random order. Again with the chalk, create a starting line approximately 30 feet (9 meters) from the Speed Count squares.

DIRECTIONS

1. Create groups of 13 to 15 students. Teams begin behind the starting line.

2. On your signal, teams approach their square. Their task is to touch the circles in sequence, 1 through 25, by sending one student at a time to touch one circle at a time. Teams get a 10-second penalty if two members enter the square at the same time.

3. Once all circles have been touched in order, the entire team returns to the starting point and the clock stops.

4. When everyone has finished, provide time for teams to develop a strategy to improve their score and then try again.

VARIATION

Substitute letters of the alphabet and give students words to spell by touching the spots in sequence.

Stump Jump

OBJECTIVES

Communication, teamwork

EQUIPMENT

3 poly spots for each pair of students, cones

SETUP

This activity requires a defined area approximately the size of a basketball court. Designate a start and end point using cones.

DIRECTIONS

1. Divide the class into pairs and provide them with three poly spots.

2. Students cross from the starting point to the other side of the playing area using the poly spots to advance. They move forward by standing on their poly spots and moving the third spot toward the other end of the playing area. Students then leap forward to the spots in front of them. They must stand on a poly spot at all times while in the playing area.

3. At the end point, the pair joins another pair. They combine poly spots so that now there are four students and six poly spots to use.

4. The new group returns to the starting point and completes the task again.

5. When they reach the end, the group of four students joins another group of four and they cross the gym floor again, now with eight participants and 12 poly spots.

6. Students continue combining groups, increasing the size of the teams and the number of poly spots until they form a group of 32.

VARIATION

At the conclusion of the activity, instruct the class to form a circle within the playing area. Students must work together to coordinate their movement and use of poly spots so everyone within the class is able to join the circle.

Freeze and Thaw

OBJECTIVES

Cardiorespiratory endurance, dodging, fleeing, agility, communication, teamwork, passing, catching

EQUIPMENT

1 foam ball for each student minus two, 2 foam noodles, 6 cones

SETUP

Use the cones to define an area approximately the size of two basketball courts.

DIRECTIONS

1. Select two students to be taggers and provide them with noodles to tag players. All other students receive a ball.
2. The taggers try to tag as many students as they can. When tagged, the students kneel on one knee and place their ball next to them.
3. Students who are tagged are frozen in place. They must extend their hands in front of them and yell "Thaw out!", trying to attract another player to toss them a ball.
4. The tosser must stand at least 3 feet (1 meter) away from the frozen player and toss the ball to the frozen player, who must catch it to be freed.
5. After catching the ball, the frozen player keeps the ball and is free to run. The tosser grabs the ball that was left by the frozen player and continues play.
6. If the ball is not caught, the tosser must retrieve it and then either try again or move on.
7. Play continues until all players are frozen or until stopped by you.

Partner Pull

OBJECTIVES

Appropriate touch, strength, balance, teamwork

EQUIPMENT

Chalk or 20-foot (6-meter) rope

SETUP

Lay the rope down in the center of the playing area, or draw a line in the center with the chalk. You may also use any line of a marked court that is long enough to accommodate the class.

DIRECTIONS

1. Divide the class into two equal groups. One group stands on one side of the rope or line and the other group stands on the other side, facing each other.

2. Students grab the hand of the person across from them. On your signal, they try to pull the other player across onto their side of the rope. Players who are pulled across stay on that side and find another opponent on the other side to challenge.

3. The game continues for approximately 2 or 3 minutes. If no opponent is available, students must wait until one is. Students choose whom to challenge. A student who is challenged may refuse but must immediately find a different person to challenge.

Hog Call

OBJECTIVES

Listening skills, communication

EQUIPMENT

1 blindfold per student (optional)

SETUP

This activity requires a well-defined area approximately the size of a tennis half-court.

DIRECTIONS

1. Place students in pairs and instruct them to create a two-word phrase or compound word they can call out to each other and identify themselves, such as baseball, catfish, sleigh-ride, yo-dude, and so on. Then they decide who will say which part of the phrase or word.

2. The pairs split up and go to opposite sides, waiting just outside of the playing area.

3. Students put their blindfolds on or close their eyes.

4. Say, "Bumpers up!" This signals students to hold their hands out in front of them while walking around the playing area.

5. When you say, "Hog call!", students enter the playing area, calling out their portion of the phrase and listening for their partner. As students approach the center of the playing area, they try to grab onto their partner's hands.

6. Once the pairs find each other, they open their eyes or remove their blindfolds and return to one end of the playing area.

VARIATIONS

- Students return to another part of the floor not directly across from their partner.
- Barnyard: Form groups of four. Students select an animal noise, like a quack, bark, whinny, and so on, and then split up to each take their place on one side of the playing area. After putting on their blindfolds, they migrate toward the center, mimicking their animal noise and trying to find their pack, herd, flock, and so on.

Canoe Race

OBJECTIVES

Communication, trust, teamwork

EQUIPMENT

4-foot (1.2-meter) pole or rope for each group of 4-6 students; various obstacles such as cones, low hurdles, or a rope stretched between two high cones for students to go around, over, and under

SETUP

In a well-defined area approximately the size of a basketball court, create an obstacle course using cones and objects for students to go around, over, and under. Make sure that it is well marked and steady enough to withstand inadvertent bumping by students.

DIRECTIONS

1. Place students in groups of 4 to 6 and provide them with a 4-foot (1.2-meter) pole or rope.
2. Students straddle the pole and hold it with both hands in front of them. The student at the front faces one way while the remaining students on the team face the other way. The front student is the driver of the team.
3. On your signal, the driver guides the remaining students through the course, calling out to them where they are going and what they must do to travel together through the course.
4. Once they've completed the course, students switch roles and try again.

VARIATION

Turn this into a partner activity, with one person facing forward, the other backward. Then partners reverse on the way back. (You can also use rope for this, but it makes it much harder to steer).

Bull-Ring Transport

OBJECTIVES

Teamwork, communication, patience, critical thinking

EQUIPMENT

8 1.5-inch (4-centimeter) bull rings (thick metal rings), 42 pieces of 4-foot (1.2-meter) twine, 8 PVC pipes 2 feet (61 centimeters) in length and 6 inches (15 centimeters) in diameter, 8 golf balls, 8 cones

SETUP

This activity requires a well-defined area approximately the size of two basketball courts. Tie six pieces of twine to each bull ring so that they extend from the ring. Place one PVC pipe in each cone. Place the cones on the opposite side of the playing area.

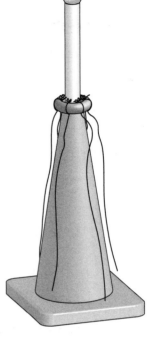

DIRECTIONS

1. Divide the class into eight teams.
2. Teams balance the golf ball on the bull ring and, using tension from the strings, transport the golf ball to a PVC pipe.
3. Students release the strings with the bull ring resting at the base of the PVC pipe so that the golf ball remains on the pipe.

VARIATIONS

- Use a plastic bottle or bowling pin in place of the golf ball.
- Create an obstacle course for students to maneuver through.
- Use different lengths of twine.
- Put a 2-foot (61-centimeter) circle around the PVC pipe that students may not cross when performing the maneuver.

Diminishing Circle

OBJECTIVES

Teamwork, communication, spatial awareness

EQUIPMENT

12-foot (3.5-meter) rope for every 6-8 students

SETUP

None

DIRECTIONS

1. Create groups of 6 to 8 students and give each group a rope.
2. Students form a circle on the floor with the rope.
3. On your signal, the group goes to the rope and enters the circle without touching one another.
4. After a few tries, time the groups. Make the circle smaller each time.

Form a Letter

OBJECTIVE

Teamwork

EQUIPMENT

Dry-erase board and markers (optional)

SETUP

This activity requires a well-defined area approximately the size of a basketball half-court.

DIRECTIONS

1. Students mingle within the boundaries of the area and wait for you to speak or write a number and letters, such as the following: 2L, 1I, 3F, 4E, 5NL, 8NFL, 7UCLA. You can use small words or acronyms that students are familiar with for fun.
2. Students form a group with the indicated number and then form the indicated letters with their bodies as quickly as possible.
   - 2L: Two students form an "L" shape
   - 7UCLA: Seven students form the letters "UCLA"
3. Once letters are formed, scan the room and highlight formations.
4. Students mingle and wait for another number and letters. Keep the pace quick but monitor students, praising creativity.
5. If a group is unable to find sufficient players, they may continue to form the letter or letters.

Dome Balance

OBJECTIVES

Body balance, partner balance, group balance

EQUIPMENT

2 heavy dome cones per student (must be able to support a person's weight and should be in various colors)

SETUP

Stack the cones in a well-defined area approximately the size of a basketball half-court.

DIRECTIONS

1. Students take a dome cone and find a space within the play area.
2. Announce a task that students must perform on their cone.

- With one person and one dome, students balance on
  - 1 foot,
  - 2 feet,
  - 1 foot and 1 hand,
  - 1 foot and 2 hands,
  - 2 feet and 2 hands,
  - abdomen, or
  - rear end (sitting).
- With one person and two domes, students balance with
  - 1 foot and 1 hand on each dome;
  - 2 feet on a dome and 2 hands on the other dome (push-up position), and then turn from push-up position to crab position;
  - 1 hand on a dome, 1 foot on the other dome;
  - rear end on a dome with feet on the other dome; or
  - rear end on a dome with hands on the other dome.
- With a partner (two people, four domes), students balance with
  - 2 hands on a dome, 2 feet on the other while partner does the same to create an X with the two bodies;
  - 4 feet on a dome, 2 hands on another, and 2 hands on another (in push-up position), and then turn over to a crab position;
  - 2 hands on a dome and 1 foot each on two domes (diamond);
  - rear end on a dome with feet on two other domes (shared feet); or
  - three domes placed around the fourth dome. Partners each place a foot on the center dome, sharing that dome and placing their other foot on different domes. They spin around only using the outer domes to balance and push off to continue spinning.
- Group domes
  - Call out colors and have large groups stand on only those colors.
  - Arrange domes in a circle so that everyone stands on two domes. The group then must move around the circle (sharing domes as needed to move).
  - Students make a one-footed statue (standing on a dome with one foot), helping each other by staying together and supporting the group.

Tarp Magic

OBJECTIVES

Communication, problem-solving skills

EQUIPMENT

1 plastic tarp for each group of 8-10 students

SETUP

Scatter the tarps around the playing area, either indoors or on grass (not on black-top).

DIRECTIONS

1. Place students in groups of 8 to 10 and assign each group to a tarp.
2. Provide the following tasks for students to perform. Students are not allowed to touch the floor with any body part (no leaving the tarp).

Activities

- Flip that tarp: Stand on the bottom of the tarp and flip it so the underneath side is now facing up. Students cannot step off the tarp.
- Stand on half, one-quarter, or one-eighth of the tarp by folding it.
- Turn the tarp into a diamond, triangle, house shape, octagon, and so on.
- Magic carpet: Move the tarp across the floor.
- Students cover as much of the tarp with their bodies as possible.
- Make an animal out of the tarp.
- Make a burrito, enchilada, or tostada (students are the fixings).
- Create a square using six tarps. (Hint: You might want the groups to come together to form the square.)

TEACHING TIP

Students figure out pretty quickly how to solve the challenges. The key is for you to be enthusiastic and supportive. Students will begin to watch others and build on each other's learning.

Squash Balls

OBJECTIVES

Teamwork, balance, cooperation

EQUIPMENT

4 tennis balls per student, masking tape

SETUP

Establish a crossing that is approximately 25 feet (7.5 meters) long on a hard surface (not grass). Mark the start and finish with strips of masking tape.

DIRECTIONS

1. Give each person four tennis balls.
2. Students stand on the tennis balls without touching the ground and try to cross the playing area. They can use a partner or others to help balance, can share tennis balls with others, and can place the balls anywhere on the floor (the balls can be moved and then used again by others).
3. If students blatantly touch the ground with any part of their body, they must return to the start.

TEACHING TIP

Stepping on the ball of the foot rather than the arch makes it easier to balance and avoid contact with the floor.

Knock It Off

OBJECTIVES

Teamwork, agility, spatial awareness

EQUIPMENT

1 table-tennis paddle or spoon and 1 table-tennis ball or piece of paper crumpled into a ball per student

SETUP

This activity requires a well-defined area approximately the size of a basketball court.

DIRECTIONS

1. Give everyone a paddle or plastic spoon and a ball.
2. Students balance the ball on their paddle while trying to knock the balls of other students off by flicking the ball with their finger and thumb.
3. If the ball is flicked off, students just pick it up and continue playing.

VARIATIONS

- Try this as a one-on-one game.
- Try this as a two-on-two game—great teamwork is needed!

Jurassic Planet

OBJECTIVES

Getting to know other students, nonverbal and verbal communication

EQUIPMENT

None

SETUP

This activity requires a well-defined area approximately the size of a basketball court.

DIRECTIONS

1. Every person starts as an egg and must walk while squatting. Eggs find other eggs to play Rock, Paper, Scissors with (see page 21 in chapter 1). The winner becomes a chick.
2. Chicks stand up, flap their arms, and chirp while finding other chicks to play Rock, Paper, Scissors with. The winning chick becomes a dinosaur and the losing chick becomes an egg again.
3. Dinosaurs stand up, take heavy steps, and roar while finding other dinosaurs to play with. The winner becomes a king, while the losing dinosaur becomes a chick.

4. Kings place their hands above their head to signify a crown. Kings challenge each other, and the winner remains a king while the loser becomes a dinosaur. Play continues for approximately 5 to 8 minutes.

Dowel Exchange

OBJECTIVES

Partner and group cooperation, timing, teamwork

EQUIPMENT

1 wooden dowel per student, 1 inch (3 centimeters) in diameter and 4 feet (1.2 meters) in length

SETUP

This activity requires an area approximately the size of a basketball half-court.

DIRECTIONS

1. Divide the class into pairs and give each student a wooden dowel.
2. Partners stand across from each other 4 feet (1.2 meters) apart. Players place the wooden dowel to their side and slightly out in front with their left hand resting on the top. This will allow one end of the dowel to rest gently on the ground in an upright position.
3. On your signal ("One, two, three, exchange"), players quickly move to the other side to grab their partner's dowel before it falls to the ground. Repeat.

VARIATIONS

- As students get better, they move one step back, creating more distance in the exchange.
- Students use the right hand to create a crisscross exchange by sending their dowel to the right hand of their partner. Dowels will cross over each other as they fall toward the partners.
- Students form a circle and exchange dowels going counterclockwise and then clockwise.
- Students form a circle. Call out the direction in which students should exchange dowels.

Houdini Hoops

OBJECTIVES

Communication, helpfulness, teamwork

EQUIPMENT

Hula hoop for each group of 6 students

SETUP

This activity requires a well-defined area approximately the size of a basketball court.

DIRECTIONS

1. Divide the class into groups of six and give each group a hula hoop.
2. Groups form a circle, join hands, and place the hoop over one person's wrist so it dangles like a bracelet.
3. On your signal, students move the hoop around the circle (right or left) by stepping and ducking through it. The object is to see how quickly they can move the hoop around the circle while not letting go of hands.

VARIATIONS

- Students see how quickly they can pass the hoop around the circle two times and then yell "Hooray!" when done.
- Students see how many times they can move the hoop around the circle in 1 minute.
- Two groups combine and move two hoops around the new circle.
- The entire group makes one big circle and passes all of the hoops.

Student-Centered Learning

"My success is measured by my willingness to keep trying."

—*Anonymous*

The MOOMBA philosophy creates a pact between students and teacher that allows students to become members of a learning community. This shift from traditional teaching strategies where the teacher demonstrates and then the students repeat what has been taught moves the students toward a learning environment where they assume responsibility for everyone's success. When this shift occurs, not only is there more time to observe student learning and provide feedback, but also the students better internalize learning because it is far more powerful and personal.

In physical education, student learning is the ability to "demonstrate understanding of movement concepts, principles, strategies, and tactics as they apply to the learning and performance of physical activities," according to NASPE national standard 2. In student-centered lessons, students are active participants in learning new skills based on previous experiences. Gone are the days when students were given a ball to play with and told to report the final score to the teacher at the end of the class. Instead, students discover new movement skills in a setting where they can experiment and challenge themselves.

NASPE national standard 2 is reprinted from *Moving into the Future: National Standards for Physical Education*, Second Edition, with permission from the National Association for Sport and Physical Education [NASPE], 1900 Association Drive, Reston, VA 20191, USA.

A major goal of physical education is to help students become curious about movement and experiment to learn new skills. Students must be willing to risk embarrassment by trying skills in which they are not proficient. This requires a learning environment that is physically, emotionally, and socially safe. Additionally, students must learn how to observe movement in order to learn new skills. Before students can become independent learners, the teacher must structure movement experiences to help them become physically aware. The creation of MOOMBA, or a positive learning environment, is essential for students to become independent learners.

A student-centered learning environment requires students to have essential learning skills:

- Be observant of self and others. This includes not only physical movement but also attitude and how students interact with others.
- Participate in the learning experience with effort. Students must try hard and do their best.
- Support student learning. Students learn how to encourage others and help guide their peers through movement experiences.
- Be persistent and positive. Students keep trying and encourage others to try their best. They don't settle for the easy way out.

Laying the Foundation

Before student-centered learning can take place, you must establish clear expectations for student behavior and build a MOOMBA classroom environment. Therefore, before beginning the units in this chapter, you should complete a unit reinforcing student and class expectations, equipment care, protocols, and procedures, as well as a unit that teaches students how to work together cooperatively (see chapter 1 for ideas). Once this has been accomplished, students are ready to move on to units that allow for greater freedom because they have successfully demonstrated that they can

- follow directions,
- move safely from place to place,
- stay on task,
- work safely with equipment, and
- encourage peer learning.

Student-centered learning through self-discovery increases student ownership in the learning process. The four units in this chapter include juggling; circus tricks; tossing, catching, throwing, and striking; and foot skills. Each is structured for students to explore movement. Students move at their own pace, challenge themselves, teach each other, and experiment. You become a facilitator who creates a safe learning environment where students can take risks and try new movement skills. Because of this laboratory-like setting, the content of this chapter is different than others. The focus is creating a space where students can do the exploring and teaching, and thus the emphasis is on introducing the lab and allowing students the freedom to explore.

The units use task cards, which allow groups of students to become peer coaches in learning a task. Take care in training students how to move from one task area to another, how to care for equipment, and how to apply safety rules when executing a task. You must be diligent in observing the class as a whole and enforcing safety rules. Once properly trained, however, students will have more opportunities to handle the equipment, experiment, and challenge themselves.

To create a task card, do the following:

- Use 8.5- × 11-inch (22- × 28-centimeter) paper. Choose colored paper if possible.
- Laminate the card for durability. Heavy lamination can be done at any office and printing center but can be expensive. However, the cards will last several years.
- Insert the card in a cone that has been slit 4 inches (10 centimeters). Alternatively, you can purchase a task-card holder through Sportime (www.sportime.com).

Unit 1: Juggling

This is a great student-centered unit that develops eye–hand coordination and tracking. It allows students to set their own pace of learning and challenge themselves. Most students do not have much experience with juggling, so everyone starts on the same playing field, allowing you to create a nurturing environment for all students to support and encourage each other. Students will practice juggling scarves, balls that do not bounce, balls that bounce, clubs, and rings.

As the teacher, you set the tone for success. Give students incentives to master more complex tasks but support them regardless of their skills through adapted use of equipment. Use the Juggling Wall of Fame to challenge students on all levels, pushing them to strive for mastery of basic and more complex skills. The Wall of Fame is a bulletin board in a central location for all students to view. Cut-out colored balls display the names of students who have achieved various levels of proficiency. Students can move up the wall by completing a certain number of tricks, as follows.

- Red level: Proficient in juggling scarves or balls; can perform three basic cascades in a row.
- Blue level: Proficient in juggling balls with seven variations.
- Gold level: Proficient in juggling balls with 14 variations.
- Platinum level: Proficient in juggling balls with 21 variations. Few students reach this level of proficiency. Because of the dedication these skills require, include a picture of the students on the platinum ball along with their name.
- Juggle Bug: Students can become Juggle Bugs, or peer teachers, once they've gained blue status. They are now certified to assist other students in reaching their desired level of proficiency.

CD-ROM Materials

Print the following posters (reproducibles 4.1 through 4.8) from the CD-ROM and hang them in the gym:

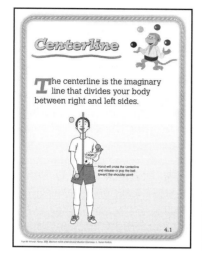

- 4.1 Centerline: Students see that the centerline bisects the body into two halves, right and left. Students use this poster as a guide to ensure they are tossing the ball across the centerline toward the opposite shoulder point.

- 4.2 Shoulder Points: Students see the target of their tosses and get an idea of the specific height and location of each toss.

- 4.3 Tray Plane: Students can see the level at which they should keep their hands to catch the objects.

- 4.4 Wall Plane: The wall plane is the imaginary wall students use to keep tosses in close proximity to their bodies. Students use the wall plane to prevent them from tossing the ball too far away from their shoulder points. Tip: Sometimes it's necessary to place students 2 feet (61 centimeters) in front of an actual wall and have them toss the ball to their shoulder points without the object hitting the wall.

As we prepare students to learn more complex juggling moves, it is important to remember not to structure the experience so tightly as to require students to master tricks in sequence as they are presented on the juggling posters. (You can also find many other juggling tricks at www.jugglingtricksunlimited.com.) Students will gravitate to one trick over another:

- 4.5 Juggling Basics and Variations: Diagrams the path and sequence of basic juggling tosses with variations for the beginner.

- 4.6 Juggling Tricks I: Diagrams the path and sequence of trick juggling moves for the intermediate juggler.

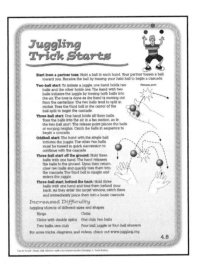

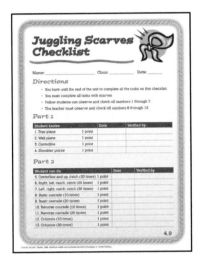

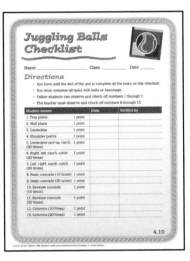

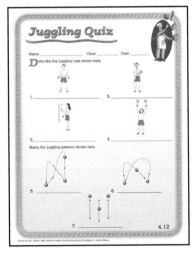

- 4.7 Juggling Tricks II: Diagrams the path and sequence of more complex juggling moves for the more advanced juggler.

- 4.8 Juggling Trick Starts: There are a variety of ways students can initiate the juggle. These are fun starts students can experiment with throughout the unit.

Print the following handouts (reproducibles 4.9 through 4.13) from the CD-ROM and distribute them to students when appropriate:

- 4.9 Juggling Scarves Checklist: This checklist is a formative assessment tool used to identify stages of growth or mastery for each student. Formative assessments help the teacher refine or revisit instruction to support student learning. Students have a clear expectation of what skills are expected for the beginning juggler. Although we would like to see all students progress to using balls, it may be necessary for students to use scarves to demonstrate the basic elements of a cascade.

- 4.10 Juggling Balls Checklist: Students use balls to demonstrate the skills required for a simple juggling rotation.

- 4.11 Juggling Report: The Juggling Report is used to help students articulate the movement concepts required to perform the psychomotor skills specific to juggling. Students write from the perspective of a person teaching juggling to another person. The report helps you assess how well the student understands how to apply the concepts toward the execution of a skill, regardless of their ability to perform the task at any given time.

- 4.12 Juggling Quiz: It is important to ensure that students know the terms that will be used throughout the lesson. Tray plane, centerline, and shoulder points will be used often throughout the unit, so students must be aware what these terms mean and identify these points in real application.

• 4.13 Juggling Wall of Fame Planning Guide: Recognition of student achievement is essential to improved participation and student growth. The Juggling Wall of Fame encourages students to challenge themselves with more complicated tricks and starts. Integrate this strategy at the beginning of the unit by introducing students to the Wall of Fame and posting the wall in a prominent place, and it becomes a key motivator for students to practice and work through the frustration that is inevitable in learning a new skill. The planning guide assists students in deciding which tricks they will incorporate into their routines.

Introductory Lesson

You do not need to demonstrate all the tricks or teach them to the students. In fact, student-centered learning requires that you refrain from showing or explaining skills beyond the basic cue points and the cascade. You will present the students with a situation that they must solve on their own using the resources provided around the room. Students see tricks on the posters and try them. They will push themselves and teach others. It's contagious! The key ingredient in the students' success is for you to be supportive, enthusiastic, and have good classroom management.

Cue Points

First, introduce and demonstrate the cue points. Students will learn four cue points in juggling.

- Centerline: Midline of the body that divides it into right and left sides. As balls are tossed from each hand, they must cross the centerline toward the shoulder point.
- Shoulder points: Target points where balls are tossed. Balls should consistently hit the shoulder points as they are tossed across the centerline.
- Tray plane: The juggling floor. Balls are caught within 6 to 8 inches (15 to 20 centimeters) of this plane.
- Wall plane: Imaginary wall that is parallel with the front of the body. Balls are not tossed beyond this wall.

Next, ask students to demonstrate them.

- Centerline: Midline of the body that divides it into right and left halves. Keep the hands on either side of the centerline. As balls are tossed from each hand, the balls cross the centerline toward the shoulder point.
- Shoulder points: Target points where balls are tossed. These are points above the shoulders approximately the length of our arms when we point with our index fingers. Toss the right ball toward the left shoulder point. Practice hitting that target. Watch each other and provide feedback on whether your partner is hitting the point. (Be encouraging! Students practice the toss with one ball only.)
- Tray plane: The juggling floor. Do not catch balls below this imaginary floor that extends along your waistline. Catch and toss the ball from the tray plane. Try not to reach for the ball; instead, allow the ball to drop to you.
- Wall plane: The imaginary wall about 2 feet (61 centimeters) in front of you. Do not toss the ball beyond this wall. Most people tend to toss the ball away from themselves. The result is called *juggler runs,* moving forward to catch the ball. Try to keep the ball within the wall plane so that you are not moving forward. It's helpful to face a wall and try to toss without hitting the wall.

Students must be able to describe and demonstrate these fundamentals, as well as use them in assessing other students' juggling. To demonstrate that they fully understand the basic movements of juggling, they develop a report on how to teach juggling. Through this progression, students learn the value of cue points and understand that mastering these cues will lead to successful juggling.

Demonstration of Tossing

Demonstrate how to toss using scarves. (You can also show a video.) Follow the steps below to demonstrate how to toss in a basic cascade (see figure 4.1). The figure shows the use of balls, but we recommend using scarves for the demonstration. Because scarves move slower than balls, students will be able to see the movements while you talk them through the process.

1. Toss and catch one scarf, reaching the opposite shoulder point and catching the scarf with the opposite hand. When you toss the scarf with the right hand, it will cross the centerline toward the left shoulder point, hitting the height of the left shoulder point, and be caught at the tray plane of the left hand. Now toss the scarf with the left hand, crossing the centerline, hitting the height of the right shoulder point, and catching the scarf with the right hand. Continue to practice, making sure to hit the height of the opposite shoulder point.

2. Toss and catch two scarves, concentrating on hitting shoulder points. After tossing the scarf from the right hand, wait for it to hit the left shoulder point before tossing the left. Keep the following rhythm: toss right, toss left, catch left, catch right (i.e., toss, toss, catch, catch).

3. Toss and catch three scarves. Start with two scarves in the right hand and one in the left. Use the pattern in step 2 and toss the third scarf when the left hand catches the first scarf (i.e., toss right, toss left, catch left, toss right, catch right).

Two additional variations can challenge students to pursue the next level on the Wall of Fame and recognition for achievement beyond the basic cascade. These variations are the reverse cascade (figure 4.2) and columns (figure 4.3). Again, the figures show the use of balls, but we recommend using scarves for the demonstration.

Use and Care of Equipment

Remind students to respect the equipment. Make pod leaders responsible for distributing equipment to students as they line up to receive the equipment of their choice. This prevents students from running to grab their equipment. At the conclusion, have students sit on their magic numbers as pod leaders collect the equipment.

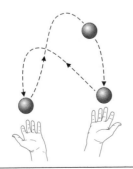

FIGURE 4.1 Basic cascade (ball crosses within the arc of the toss).

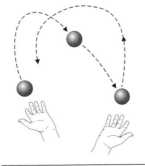

FIGURE 4.2 Reverse cascade (ball crosses outside the arc of the toss).

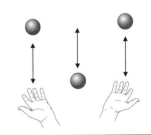

FIGURE 4.3 Columns (inside ball moves in the opposite direction of outside balls).

Class Management

Students can move freely from station to station, so there will be much activity and movement without teacher direction. To be successful in a student-centered environment, students must be able to stop, sit, and listen when you direct them to do so. Here is where the activities from chapter 1 really pay off—you will be able to stop class activity to give instructions or the next steps.

Assessment

Provide students with a checklist to keep track of their accomplishments, progress, and upcoming challenges. Make sure students are aware that they must perform a basic cascade using scarves or balls at the conclusion of the unit. In addition, students are expected to know the patterns for the reverse cascade and columns, although they do not have to perform them.

Recognition

Post a Juggling Wall of Fame in the main hall or some other central place for the school to view. As discussed earlier, students can earn recognition for higher levels of achievement. You can also give students the Juggling Wall of Fame Planning Guide so they can chart their progress. (See reproducible 4.13 on the CD-ROM.)

Organization of the Juggling Unit

Create three stations where students can practice. At the first station, students use scarves; at the second station they use balls; and at the last they are introduced to tricks with balls, clubs, and rings. At all stations, mount juggling posters on the wall that describe cue points, juggling variations, and assessment levels. Play juggling videos at all three stations, moving students from introduction and practice to juggling three balls.

Do not force students to practice at specific stations or to follow a required progression or assessment. The students choose where to begin, when to move to a higher level, and how far to challenge themselves. Remind students that they will be assessed and that at a minimum they are expected to perform a basic cascade with balls or scarves. Have students try to complete one cycle and practice this sequence until all tosses are in control (i.e., no juggling runs or grabbing above the tray plane) before moving up to two cycles.

Assess students on their ability to complete at least 10 rotations of a basic cascade. You can assess them at any time during the unit. Students form groups with others at the same proficiency or find Juggle Bugs to assist them through a juggling pattern. Because this is a student-centered lesson, students form their own groups with your encouragement rather than your directive.

Unit 2: Circus Tricks

In this unit, students are placed in small groups and must perform a task at a station for a certain length of time before moving to the next station. The circus tricks involve equipment that requires students to adhere to basic safety precautions. Therefore, it is critical that you spend the first day demonstrating each station, proper care and use of the equipment, any safety considerations, and how to move safely from station to station. This orientation should not be rushed and students must be attentive.

In addition, it's your job to monitor the class and facilitate movement and safe use of the equipment during the lesson. After each rotation, students must go down on one knee and place equipment the way they found it before you allow them to rotate to the next station. This gives you the opportunity to scan the room to ensure that the equipment is in good working order, holds students accountable for the care of equipment since they know you are going to check it after each use, and leaves the station organized for the next group. Require students to examine the equipment when they arrive at a station and report to you immediately if there is any damage or missing parts (for example, the rubber cap on the end of a stilt).

This unit must be held indoors because it requires a controlled environment. Wind can make the use of some equipment difficult. Additionally, the indoor environment helps you monitor students and reinforce positive student behavior. Recognize students who are proficient in a station by designating them as a junior teacher. These students are available to assist other students by demonstrating a trick or coaching the skills.

See figure 4.4 for a sample setup for the circus stations. The stations in this unit focus on developing a variety of psychomotor skills. Students have several movement experiences at varying levels of difficulty. Following are the categories of movement skills and their corresponding activities.

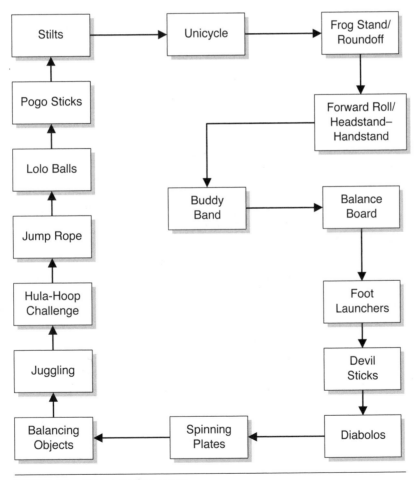

FIGURE 4.4 Circus station setup.

Frog Stand

1. Triangle balance between your head and hands.
2. Place your weight evenly on your head and hands.
3. Hold for 15 seconds.
4. Try a tripod by simply holding the position and then slowly lifting your head off the floor and balancing.

4.14

Roundoff

1. Lunge and lever with squared hips: Bring legs together in the air, then snap the legs down, keeping them straight.
2. Hands come off the ground before the feet touch the ground.
3. Only one person should be on the mat if performing a cartwheel or roundoff.

4.15

Headstand

1. Triangle balance between your head and hands.
2. Roll legs up to your chest and begin extending your legs overhead.
3. Your legs should be straight and your body slightly slanted.
4. Keep a safe distance from other tumblers.

4.16

Handstand

1. Face a wall, standing about an arm's length away.
2. Place your hands on the floor, halfway between you and the wall.
3. Support your body weight with your hands as you lift your legs above your head.
4. Have your heels touch the wall for balance if necessary, but try to balance by yourself without the support of the wall.
5. When you get tired or start to lose your balance, quickly bring your knees to your chest and roll away from the wall.

4.17

Forward Roll

1. Tuck your chin to your chest.
2. Have your shoulders touch the ground.
3. Stand up without using your hands.

4.18

Balance and Tumbling

Balance and tumbling help students become more aware of their bodies and how they move through space. The following activities are basic movement skills that allow students to work on personal flexibility, strength, and balance. (See reproducibles 4.14 through 4.23 on the CD-ROM.)

- 4.14 Frog Stand: Students remain in a tucked position as they bring their feet over their bodies, balancing on three points using their heads and knees. Students do not extend their legs.

- 4.15 Roundoff: Students begin a cartwheel, but while their hands make contact with the ground their feet come together and they perform a snapping motion with their waist to bring both feet to the ground simultaneously.

- 4.16 Headstand: Students use three points of contact with the ground—the head and both hands. Students extend both feet above their body.

- 4.17 Handstand: Students extend both feet above their body with only two points of contact with the ground—their right and left hands.

- 4.18 Forward Roll: Students crouch down in a frog stance with their weight evenly distributed between their feet and hands. Then they transfer their weight onto their hands and lean forward. Students place their head on the ground while pushing off with their feet and propelling themselves forward with their hands. Safety tip: It is important for students to understand that their legs and hands push them forward and that they shouldn't place their full body weight on the head. Watch students perform this task, and have a spotter help them keep their movement forward. Not moving forward results in the head and neck bearing the weight of the body during rotation.

- 4.19 Balance Board: The balance board is a 2-foot by 8-inch (61- by 20-centimeter) board that is placed over a cylinder. The student places each foot on the end of the board, creating a fulcrum in the middle of the board. The student tries to balance the board so that

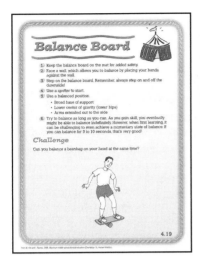

Balance Board

1. Keep the balance board on the mat for added safety.
2. Face a wall, which allows you to balance by placing your hands against the wall.
3. Step on the balance board. Remember, always step on and off the downside!
4. Use a spotter to start.
5. Use a balanced position.
   - Broad base of support
   - Lower center of gravity (lower hips)
   - Arms extended out to the side
6. Try to balance as long as you can. As you gain skill, you eventually might be able to balance indefinitely. However, when first learning, it can be challenging to even achieve a momentary state of balance. If you can balance for 5 to 10 seconds, that's very good!

Challenge

Can you balance a beanbag on your head at the same time?

4.19

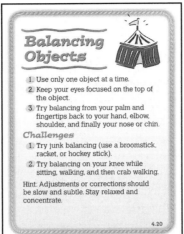

Balancing Objects

1. Use only one object at a time.
2. Keep your eyes focused on the top of the object.
3. Try balancing from your palm and fingertips back to your hand, elbow, shoulder, and finally your nose or chin.

Challenges

1. Try junk balancing (use a broomstick, racket, or hockey stick).
2. Try balancing on your knee while sitting, walking, and then crab walking.

Hint: Adjustments or corrections should be slow and subtle. Stay relaxed and concentrate.

4.20

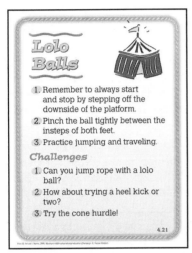

Lolo Balls

1. Remember to always start and stop by stepping off the downside of the platform.
2. Pinch the ball tightly between the insteps of both feet.
3. Practice jumping and traveling.

Challenges

1. Can you jump rope with a lolo ball?
2. How about trying a heel kick or two?
3. Try the cone hurdle!

4.21

Pogo Sticks

1. Keep the stick hugged tightly to your waist and legs.
2. Practice jumping up and down in the chalked circle.
3. Practice traveling from one circle to the other.

Challenges

1. Try a tire maze.
2. Try jumping a cone hurdle.
3. Try heel kicks.

Try to keep the pogo stick from falling to the floor!

4.22

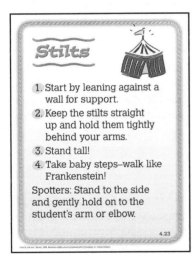

Stilts

1. Start by leaning against a wall for support.
2. Keep the stilts straight up and hold them tightly behind your arms.
3. Stand tall!
4. Take baby steps–walk like Frankenstein!

Spotters: Stand to the side and gently hold on to the student's arm or elbow.

4.23

it is level with the ground. Safety tip: Initially place students on a mat that is placed against a wall or with a student holding the hands of the student on the balance board. The mat slows the reaction of the cylinder, and the wall or student spotter helps keep the balance of the student who is on the balance board.

- 4.20 Balancing Objects: Students vertically balance a variety of long objects—broom, feather, stick, bat—on their hands.

- 4.21 Lolo Balls: A lolo ball is a rubber ball secured in a plastic platform. Students use their legs to press against the ball and balance on the platform so that only the southern hemisphere of the ball below the platform is making contact with the ground. Students are able to bend their legs and push off the ball to create a bouncing movement. Students can bounce on the lolo ball, making it move in various directions. For added challenge, place a hurdle in this station (made with two cones and a plastic stick suspended between them) and ask the student to try to jump over the hurdle using the lolo ball.

- 4.22 Pogo Sticks: Use chalk to mark 5-foot-diameter (1.5 meters) circles to create a boundary for students to perform this task. This boundary contains the movement of students and prevents them from interfering with other students performing this skill. If you are unable to mark the ground, then use cones to outline the space. As students progress, create a maze for students to move through to challenge their skills. Safety tip: Make sure students check equipment before use. In this case, train students to check the rubber tip of the pogo stick to ensure it is not damaged or missing. A direct pole-to-ground contact can make the pogo stick slip upon impact.

- 4.23 Stilts: Students balance and move on stilts. Students practice using the implements to perform a task we take for granted, walking. It is important that students bring the stilts into their body and use them as an extension of their legs to remain balanced.

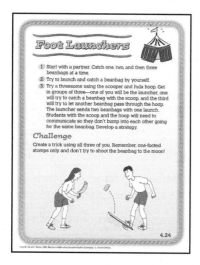

Action–Reaction

In the following activities, students learn about one of Newton's laws—every action has an equal and opposite reaction. They are interactive and fun, especially the Buddy Band. (See reproducibles 4.24 through 4.26 on the CD-ROM.)

- 4.24 Foot Launchers: Students use a lever, like a seesaw, to send objects into the air. An object is placed on one end of the lever, the end in the down position. The raised end is stepped on by the student, catapulting the object upward. Students try to catch the object.

- 4.25 Hula Hoop Challenge: Students experiment with manipulating a hula hoop. Students spin, jump through, and juggle hula hoops in this station that focuses on action–reacton laws of motion. Students use extremities to spin the hula hoop, apply backspin to the hula hoop, and try to juggle multiple hoops.

- 4.26 Buddy Band: A buddy band is a large rubber band for kids. The elastic circle is strong enough to support four students moving from corner to corner once stretched. Students must learn to communicate and coordinate their movements to fully experience the slingshot effect of the buddy band. To begin, you need four students to equally distribute themselves within the buddy band to create a square. Each student is within the band and raises the band to waist level. Each student walks backward until they are able to slightly lean their back against the band, creating a square. The students directly across from each other simultaneously lean against the band to propel themselves forward and exchange places. Once they arrive at the opposite corner, they turn and lean against the band. This tension is timed to correspond with the release of the other two students. The result is a slingshot effect that propels the students toward their opposite corner. Safety tip: Although the buddy band is durable, it is not indestructible. Stronger, larger students must be mindful of the tension and not exert so much force as to break the band.

Manipulating Objects

Manipulating objects are some of the most challenging stations in the Circus Tricks unit because they require a variety of skills to master. However, they are also the most rewarding. Here we can see the greatest amount of growth as students gain control over their objects and are able to perform a variety of tricks with them. Students who gain mastery over a particular station are eligible to be junior teachers, serving as coaches for students who need additional coaching, spotting, or tips to succeed. The teacher identifies junior teachers as students perform. A junior teacher is recognized by placing a badge or their name on a board. Students know to find a junior teacher to assist them, or the teacher may elect to place a junior teacher at a station to assist other students. Tip: A good strategy is to designate a day when junior teachers are available rather than making them available throughout the unit. This allows time for junior teachers to explore other stations

Devil Sticks

1. Practice a two-stick pickup. Holding the top end of the devil stick, practice a side-to-side, tick-tock toss while the bottom end stands or rests on the floor. Remember to softly absorb the devil stick and push away.
2. Do one-stick spinners by turning your hand and wrist quickly on the top end of the devil stick. You should be able to twirl the devil stick in a clockwise direction.
3. Keep your hand sticks parallel with the floor (horizontal).
4. See junior teachers for a demonstration and help.

Challenges
1. Try a spin, toss the devil stick in the air, and catch with two sticks.
2. Try a partner toss and catch.
3. Create your own trick!

4.27

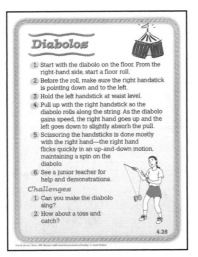

Diabolos

1. Start with the diabolo on the floor. From the right-hand side, start a floor roll.
2. Before the roll, make sure the right handstick is pointing down and to the left.
3. Hold the left handstick at waist level.
4. Pull up with the right handstick so the diabolo rolls along the string. As the diabolo gains speed, the right hand goes up and the left goes down to slightly absorb the pull.
5. Scissoring the handsticks is done mostly with the right hand—the right hand flicks quickly in an up-and-down motion, maintaining a spin on the diabolo.
6. See a junior teacher for help and demonstrations.

Challenges
1. Can you make the diabolo sing?
2. How about a toss and catch?

4.28

Spinning Plates

1. Start first with the Spin Jammer. Practice a one- and two-handed spin toss on a 2-foot-long (61 centimeters) pole. Be a balanced spinner and use both hands. Spin the plate on top of the wooden stick.
2. Practice flat tosses.
3. Keep your eye on the top of the pole!

Challenges
1. Catch and toss Spin Jammers under your leg, behind your back, and from one partner to another.
2. Try the same tricks with plates and poles.

Please be careful using the pointed poles!

4.29

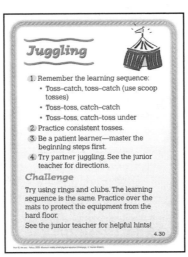

Juggling

1. Remember the learning sequence:
   • Toss–catch, toss–catch (use scoop tosses)
   • Toss–toss, catch–catch
   • Toss–toss, catch–toss under
2. Practice consistent tosses.
3. Be a patient learner—master the beginning steps first.
4. Try partner juggling. See the junior teacher for directions.

Challenge

Try using rings and clubs. The learning sequence is the same. Practice over the mats to protect the equipment from the hard floor.

See the junior teacher for helpful hints!

4.30

and play. (See reproducibles 4.27 through 4.30 on the CD-ROM.)

- 4.27 Devil Sticks: Three sticks are used in this station. Two are held as an extension of the student's hands, and the third is tossed from side to side, spun around, or tossed as if it was moving of its own accord. The key concept for students to learn is how to absorb the impact of the stick and propel it as directed in a controlled fashion.

- 4.28 Diabolos: A diabolo is an object that can be suspended on a string made taut by two held sticks. The diabolo has two half circles connected by a metal bar. The string is placed between the circles, but in order for the diabolo to balance, it must maintain a spinning motion, much like a yo-yo. Students learn how to pick up the diabolo only using the implements. The implement is placed under the diabolo and raised until the diabolo is resting on the string. With one stick pointed toward the ground, the other flicks quickly in an up-and-down motion, slightly raising and lowering the diabolo to create backspin. Once the momentum increases, the diabolo can easily be raised as it is balancing on the string. The flicking motion must be repeated as the diabolo prepares for or returns from a toss. Once a diabolo is spinning, the friction of the spinning diabolo against the string creates a whining sound; this is called "making the diabolo sing."

- 4.29 Spinning Plates: Somewhat flexible poles are used. Plastic spinning plates can be purchased that have a slight indentation on the bottom that helps balance the plate on the pole while spinning. Students practice spinning the plate on the pole and holding the pole, keeping the plate balanced. Students use their hands to spin the plate without knocking it off the pole they are holding. Once students feel comfortable manipulating the plates, students practice catching and tossing the Spin Jammer under their legs, behind their backs, or between partners during a spinning routine.

- 4.30 Juggling: Students practice juggling, using different objects including tennis balls, juggling pins, or a combination of both. Beginners can use scarves. Tip: It is best to introduce juggling before the circus tricks unit. Students enjoy returning to juggling and can experiment with different objects or reinforce what they have learned.

Tricks

The tricks section challenges students to try something new within these two stations. The first station, Jump Rope, provides students with many different variations to a skill they probably already know well. They can experiment with the variations as an individual or with a group. The unicycle station is unique in that the majority of students may have never tried to ride on a unicycle before. Here is where students can rely on others to try something new in a supportive environment. (See reproducibles 4.31 and 4.32 on the CD-ROM.)

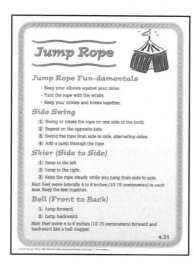

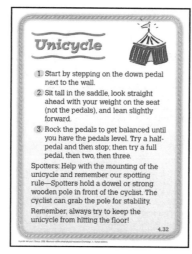

- 4.31 Jump Rope: Students perform different challenges with a jump rope, individual and group.

- 4.32 Unicycle: In order for students to be successful riding a unicycle for four or more pumps of the legs, they need to be aware of balance, action–reaction, and coordination. Here all the principles learned in the circus tricks unit come into play. It is important that students serving as spotters take their role seriously. In this station, spotters provide stability to the rider, who tries to move him- or herself forward on the unicycle. This activity requires patience and practice but is a thrill when successful.

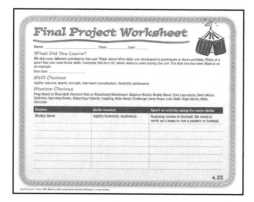

Final Project

While participating in the Circus Tricks unit, students learn about agility, balance, speed, strength, eye–hand coordination, eye–foot coordination, flexibility, and endurance. Students are asked to list the stations of the Circus Tricks unit, what skills were required to complete the task, and what sport or activity requires those same skills. (See reproducible 4.33, "Final Project Worksheet," on the CD-ROM.)

Unit 3: Tossing, Throwing, Catching, and Striking

In this unit, the physical education classroom serves as a science lab. It is the ultimate in student-centered learning: Task execution is open-ended discovery, and the lesson is performed in an open field where you are not in close proximity to the students. It's an excellent unit to integrate with a science class. Meet with a science teacher and find out when your students will be studying velocity, centrifugal force, trajectory, and inertia. Share your task cards with a science teacher you enjoy working with and see what scientific lab assignments you can assist with in your physical education class. The science teacher can create a lab sheet to accompany the task cards and review the results of the lab during science class.

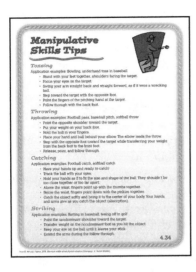

Skills

Working with manipulatives is common in sport activities. Tossing, throwing, catching, and striking an object are skills that must be taught and practiced in order for students to become highly proficient. Following are some basic principles to follow for the successful execution of these skills. (See reproducible 4.34, "Manipulative Skills Tips," on the CD-ROM.)

Tossing

Application examples: Bowling, underhand toss in baseball

- Stand with your feet together, shoulders facing the target.
- Focus your eyes on the target.
- Swing your arm straight back and straight forward, as if it were a wrecking ball.
- Step toward the target with the opposite foot.
- Point the fingers of the pitching hand at the target.
- Follow through with the back foot.

Throwing

Application examples: Football pass, baseball pitch, softball throw

- Point the opposite shoulder toward the target.
- Put your weight on your back foot.
- Hold the ball in your fingers.
- Place your hand and ball behind your elbow. The elbow leads the throw.
- Step with the opposite foot toward the target while transferring your weight from the back foot to the front foot.
- Release, point, and follow through.

Catching

Application examples: Football catch, softball catch

- Have your hands up and ready to catch!
- Track the ball with your eyes.
- Hold your hands as if to fit the size and shape of the ball. They shouldn't be too close together or too far apart.
- Above the waist, fingers point up with the thumbs together.
- Below the waist, fingers point down with the pinkies together.
- Catch the object softly and bring it to the center of your body. Your hands and arms give as you catch the object (absorption).

Striking

Application examples: Batting in baseball, teeing off in golf

- Point the nondominant shoulder toward the target.
- Transfer weight on the nondominant foot as you hit the object.
- Keep your eye on the ball until it leaves your stick.
- Extend the arms during the follow-through.

CD-ROM Materials

Print out these station directions (reproducibles 4.35 through 4.50) from the CD-ROM and hang them at the appropriate stations for students. It will also be helpful for students if you make reproducible 4.34, "Manipulative Skills Tips," available for them at each station.

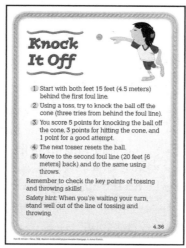

- 4.35 Target Throw: Students throw at a target and earn points for accuracy. Distance is increased to add difficulty.

- 4.36 Knock It Off: Students throw to knock items off a cone. This activity is similar to Target Throw but is more challenging and more exciting when students successfully knock an object off the cone.

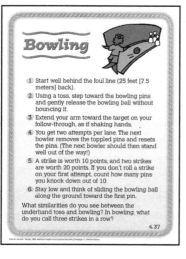

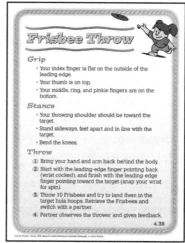

- 4.37 Bowling: Students practice tossing skills by trying to knock as many bowling pins down as possible. If desired, score could be kept at this station.

- 4.38 Frisbee Throw: Students toss Frisbees into a hula hoop from various distances.

- 4.39 Can It: Students must have good eye–hand coordination to bounce a ball and catch it on its descent in a cylinder. This activity takes practice and fine motor adjustments.

- 4.40 Above the Line: Students must catch a ball that is tossed "above the line," a horizontal line on a wall that is marked approximately 6 feet (2 meters) above the ground. Students try to toss and catch with the free hand behind their back. Increase the challenge by performing with the nondominant hand.

Throton

1. With a partner, stand opposite each other on the field space marked for throwing. Stand 20 feet (6 meters) apart.
2. Grip the middle portion of the Throton with your fingers spread apart.
3. Release the Throton off your fingertips with a snap of the wrist to get a spiral motion.
4. Pretend a rope runs through the middle of the Throton and throw along the rope. Can you throw it without it wobbling? Can you catch the Throton with one hand? If so, how many times?

Remember the key points of throwing skills!

4.41

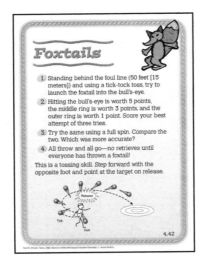

Foxtails

1. Standing behind the foul line (50 feet [15 meters]) and using a tick-tock toss, try to launch the foxtail into the bull's-eye.
2. Hitting the bull's-eye is worth 5 points, the middle ring is worth 3 points, and the outer ring is worth 1 point. Score your best attempt of three tries.
3. Try the same using a full spin. Compare the two. Which was more accurate?
4. All throw and all go—no retrieves until everyone has thrown a foxtail!

This is a tossing skill. Step forward with the opposite foot and point at the target on release.

4.42

- 4.41 Throton: With an overarm throwing motion, students toss the object for distance while achieving a spiral, like a football.
- 4.42 Foxtails: Students learn about centrifugal force and timing by tossing the foxtail for accuracy.

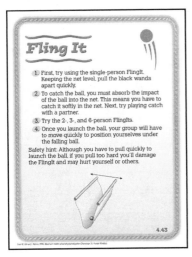

Fling It

1. First, try using the single-person FlingIt. Keeping the net level, pull the black wands apart quickly.
2. To catch the ball, you must absorb the impact of the ball into the net. This means you have to catch it softly in the net. Next, try playing catch with a partner.
3. Try the 2-, 3-, and 6-person FlingIts.
4. Once you launch the ball, your group will have to move quickly to position yourselves under the falling ball.

Safety hint: Although you have to pull quickly to launch the ball, if you pull too hard you'll damage the FlingIt and may hurt yourself or others.

4.43

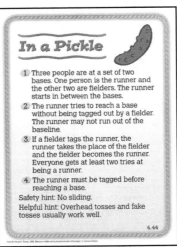

In a Pickle

1. Three people are at a set of two bases. One person is the runner and the other two are fielders. The runner starts in between the bases.
2. The runner tries to reach a base without being tagged out by a fielder. The runner may not run out of the baseline.
3. If a fielder tags the runner, the runner takes the place of the fielder and the fielder becomes the runner. Everyone gets at least two tries at being a runner.
4. The runner must be tagged before reaching a base.

Safety hint: No sliding.
Helpful hint: Overhead tosses and fake tosses usually work well.

4.44

- 4.43 Fling It: Students have fun projecting objects into the air and catching them with the FlingIt.
- 4.44 In a Pickle: Students refine their tossing and throwing skills in an isolated game of pickle.

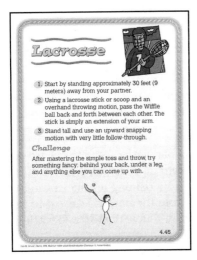

Lacrosse

1. Start by standing approximately 30 feet (9 meters) away from your partner.
2. Using a lacrosse stick or scoop and an overhand throwing motion, pass the Wiffle ball back and forth between each other. The stick is simply an extension of your arm.
3. Stand tall and use an upward snapping motion with very little follow-through.

Challenge

After mastering the simple toss and throw, try something fancy: behind your back, under a leg, and anything else you can come up with.

4.45

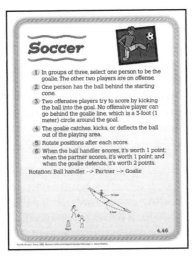

Soccer

1. In groups of three, select one person to be the goalie. The other two players are on offense.
2. One person has the ball behind the starting cone.
3. Two offensive players try to score by kicking the ball into the goal. No offensive player can go behind the goalie line, which is a 3-foot (1 meter) circle around the goal.
4. The goalie catches, kicks, or deflects the ball out of the playing area.
5. Rotate positions after each score.
6. When the ball handler scores, it's worth 1 point; when the partner scores, it's worth 1 point; and when the goalie defends, it's worth 2 points.

Rotation: Ball handler --> Partner --> Goalie

4.46

- 4.45 Lacrosse: Students use the lacrosse stick in an overarm throwing motion to throw a ball to a partner. Students also develop their skills in catching an object with a manipulative.
- 4.46 Soccer: Students refine and practice their dribbling skills to score a goal.

- 4.47 Lasso: Students love to pretend they're back in the Old West with this activity. Students use a lasso to toss over the head of a wooden horse.

- 4.48 Striking With a Bat: Students swing at a ball on a tee or cone, focusing on proper technique and form.

- 4.49 Slugger: Students hit the ball off a tee for distance.

- 4.50 Football Throw: Students throw a football for form, trying to achieve a perfect spiral.

Unit 4: Foot Skills

Students who have the greatest ability to manipulate and control the ball have the greatest success advancing the ball during play. This unit will focus on ball manipulation and control using eye–foot coordination. Students have a choice of three types of equipment when attempting to accomplish the challenges.

- Beginners can use a tethered tennis ball, or a tennis ball with a 4-foot (1.2-meter) tether that allows them to maintain control of ball flight and minimize frustration. (You can easily make a tethered tennis ball yourself by drilling a hole through a tennis ball and threading a rope through it.) Players hold the ball and drop it to the foot to execute the move. With a tethered ball, they don't have to stop and retrieve the ball when they kick it out of the control zone.

- Intermediate students can use a training Hacky Sack, footbag, or soccer ball. The footbag is larger than the Hacky Sack and is filled with foam.

- Advanced students can use a regulation footbag or soccer ball.

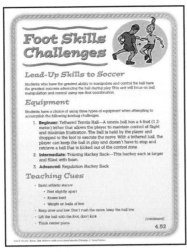

Teaching Cues

Following are general principles to tell students how to properly execute foot skills.

- Take the basic athletic stance.
  - Feet slightly apart
  - Knees bent
  - Weight on balls of the feet
- Keep slow and low. (Don't rush the move, and keep the ball low.)
- Lift (don't kick) the ball with the foot.
- Think of the centerline: Imagine a centerline dividing your body. The goal is to maintain control of the footbag within the control area. Eventually, the ball will pass from the left to the right, across the centerline. The foot will stop the direction of the ball. If the ball is coming toward the right side, the right foot will stop the motion and send it toward the left foot. The left foot will then stop the direction of the bag and return it to the right foot. Keep the ball low.

Getting Started

Eye–foot skills require practice. Like the juggling unit, creating an environment that allows students to explore, challenge themselves, and support each other in learning will determine how successful students will be. Recognize students for their achievements, provide modified equipment to ensure maximum repetitions and early success, and be encouraging and supportive as students test their skills and try new ones.

Print out forms from the CD-ROM and demonstrate the kicks (inside kick, outside kick, toe kick, knee kick, and back heel kick) to the class. The assessment sheet is a checklist students can use to check off what they have accomplished. (See reproducibles 4.51, "Foot Skills," 4.52, "Foot Skills Challenges," and 4.53, "Foot Skills Assessment," on the CD-ROM.)

Beginner Level

Start with kicks without the bag (shadowing), and use all kicks. In other words, students perform the task by pretending to receive an imaginary ball. For each kick on the list, do the following after a shadow session:

- Drop the bag or tethered tennis ball while executing an inside kick (kick–catch, kick–catch) using the same foot.
- Next, try sustaining kicks. First try three kicks in a row, then five, and so on. Push yourself! Then switch feet.
- Alternate kicking the ball from foot to foot. Keep slow and low.
- Go freestyle—use a combination of kicks.
- Try this trick—toss the ball onto your forehead or back and hold it in place. Then toss the ball back into play without using your hands.
- Do partner kicks—pass with a partner, seeing how long you can keep the ball alive.

Intermediate Level

Students perform the same activities as at the beginner level, only with a training soccer ball or regular soccer ball.

Students also try to lift the ball from the ground and begin kicking it.

- Backward roll lift: Students add backspin to a stationary ball and immediately place their foot under the ball as it rolls up on their foot.
- Passing to a partner: Students pass the ball to a partner, either on the ground or in the air. The partner must try to lift the ball with the foot to begin kicking it.

Advanced Level

Students advance from intermediate skills by adding three combinations of kicks before passing to a partner. Students are able to complete four passes to a partner.

Summary

Student-centered learning helps students become independent learners and experiment with movement skills. It also allows you to facilitate learning for a wide range of skills while challenging every child. It requires preparation of the playing area as well as a movement lab setting. You will find it exciting to see how far students can go when they are in charge of their own learning.

Sequence Learning

"The true object of all human life is play."

—G.K. Chesterton

A learning environment that focuses on maximum participation with a purpose is fundamental to maximum middle school physical education. Throughout this book we've discussed how to create a MOOMBA environment that engages students and promotes active learning. However, units on team sports, gladiator games, and rhythm and dance are especially challenging because students have such a wide range of skills. The most experienced students dominate the activity and discourage the less experienced students from participating.

This chapter presents instructional strategies that will allow you to create a MOOMBA environment in these situations. The team sport unit uses grids to set up small learning environments that isolate team skills, maximizing participation by every student. Gladiator games allow students to apply psychomotor principles—center of gravity, balance, agility, and so on—through movement games and challenges. The rhythm and dance unit creates a safe environment where all students not only participate but also contribute to the final dance project. Every student is involved in learning the skills and receives a thrill from contributing to the group's accomplishment.

Unit 1: Using Grids in Team Sport

In team sport, there is nothing more satisfying than developing the camaraderie found within a highly functioning team. Dual and team sports allow students to work cooperatively to achieve a goal, but to be successful, students must have mastery of specific movement skills and knowledge of offensive and defensive strategies. Students develop skills through multiple practice opportunities and apply them to situations that progress from simple to complex. The dilemma lies in maximizing students' participation as they learn, practice, and implement offensive and defensive strategies found in team sports such as hockey, football, basketball, and soccer.

Grids provide a way to teach the offensive and defensive skills required for a successful team. They also allow you to manage any size class while maximizing practice repetitions for every student. In this chapter, we will focus on using grids to allow students to practice isolated movements in varying degrees of proficiency. The biomechanics of these skills are beyond the scope of this book, but there is an abundance of reference materials describing this information. We recommend the following books if you're interested in learning more:

- *Teaching Middle School Physical Education: A Standards-Based Approach for Grades 5-8, Second Edition,* by Bonnie S. Mohnsen
- *Quality Lesson Plans for Secondary Physical Education, Second Edition,* by Dorothy Zakrajsek, Lois Carnes, and Frank Pettigrew, Jr.
- *Children Moving: A Reflective Approach to Teaching Physical Education, Sixth Edition,* by George Graham, Shirley Anne Holt/Hale, and Melissa Parker

Grids are rectangular or square playing areas divided into four sections. You can set up a grid simply by placing cones at the outer corners. The size of the grid varies depending on the activity, game, or number of players using the space. The goal is to ensure that all students are moving through space using basic principles required of team play. Students are assigned to groups of three or more and given a task to perform at the grid.

Creating small learning centers allows students to

- learn basic motor movements,
- learn to move to an open space within the grid,
- develop motor skills and basic team play while moving with or without an object, and
- practice defensive and offensive principles.

In this unit, the grid activities are taught in a progression, from easier activities to more challenging activities. This structure allows you to incorporate different skills within the same grid. For example, the Four Corners activity (page 52) could involve a basketball chest pass or bounce pass, or it could be converted to soccer or football. The idea is to use the formation and movement to focus on principles that are common within team sport. Basketball skills usually require smaller grids than skills required for soccer, hockey, or football.

Before implementing grid activities, it's important to consider a few guidelines that apply to all activities.

Class Management Guidelines

Following are simple protocols students should follow whenever they enter the activity area. These simple, easy-to-remember rules allow students to immediately begin play.

- **Rule of play:** Players must stay 3 feet (1 meter) away from their opponent, a player can hold the ball for no more than 3 seconds, and players must attempt to complete three passes (unless otherwise stated).

Adapted from Rule of Three from SPARK.

- **Pinnies start:** In activities that involve offense and defense, students wearing pinnies always begin with possession, and they always set up at the same end of the field. This eliminates the discussion of which team will choose an end zone and who will be offense and defense.
- **End-line scoring:** With field activities, it's better to have students attempt to score by crossing an end line than by putting the ball or object in a goal. This prevents defensive players from clustering around a goal to prevent a team from scoring, and it maximizes play for all students.

Offensive and Defensive Principles

Students will implement some basic offensive and defensive principles as they begin working in grids. It's important to isolate specific skills they need to perform in order to gain mastery.

- **Move to an open space:** Probably the most difficult offensive principle to teach young students is spreading the offense and moving to an open space.
- **Use a 45-degree angle:** Movement of the ball is more effective if tosses are at a 45-degree angle. Zigzag movement down the field is more effective because it creates more offensive options. Students can fake, change directions, or move down the field.
- **Receive at the sidelines:** When attempting to receive a ball, students should move toward the sidelines. Offensive movement toward the sidelines allows the passer to throw at a 45-degree angle and provides more options for an offensive team to move the ball.
- **Stay open:** As soon as students release the ball, they should move to an open space. If defenders block a passing lane, they can fake and move to another open space, maximizing the 45-degree angles. Whenever possible, they should look to see if they can free an offensive teammate by blocking the movement of that person's defender.

FIGURE 5.1 Passing grid.

- **Pass to the passing grid:** When passing a ball to an offensive player, students should not pass the ball to the trunk of the body. Instead, they should try to pass the ball to one of the four sections of the passing grid (figure 5.1). This placement makes it more difficult to defend and easier to catch.

- **Cover your opponent:** When trying to cover a player on the other team, students should watch and follow the belly button and stay on the balls of their feet. They should beware of fakes and react quickly by moving side to side without crossing their legs.

- **Use passing lanes:** Students on defense should try to keep their hands or implements in the passing lanes to prevent easy passes between offensive players. Offensive players should remember to pass to the passing grid, not directly to the receiver's core.

This section presents five basic grid activities: moving to open space, leading the passer, moving without the ball, playing defense, and moving with the ball. These activities can be adapted to basketball, football, team handball, ultimate Frisbee, soccer, hockey, or other team sports.

Grid activities adapted from J. Hichwa, *Right fielders are people too: An inclusive approach to teaching middle school physical education* (Champaign, IL: Human Kinetics).

Grid Activity 1: Moving to Open Space

Students learn about basic offensive strategies with and without the ball. They realize how to utilize space to balance the offense or to overload an area, creating more options for the passer.

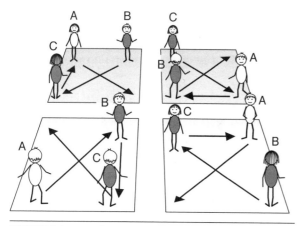

FIGURE 5.2 Moving to open space without a ball.

Without a Ball

Assign three students to a grid (see figure 5.2). The student opposite of the vacant corner begins movement by moving to the opposite corner. The other two players must decide which player will assume the spot just vacated by the first player. The third player then takes the place of the second player. Movement continues with the student opposite of the vacant corner moving to that position.

Variations: Using the same movement patterns, students move using the following skills:

- Sidestep: Students begin to use a defensive stance (figure 5.3) and pivot on the lead foot when reaching the corner. See pivoting instructions later in this section.

- Backward: Students learn to keep their eye on the offensive or defensive player while maintaining a sense of space.

Stopping

There are two types of stopping: the stride stop (also known as the *two-foot stop* or the *screech stop*) and the jump stop.

- The stride stop involves a one–two count. The forward or stopping foot is slapped down hard on the court. The body must be lowered and the stopping leg flexed as the stop occurs. The rear foot comes forward and ahead of the stopping foot to maintain

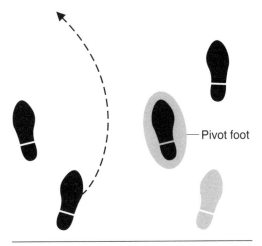

FIGURE 5.3 Sidestep.

balance. The stopping foot (now the rear foot) is the pivot foot if possession of the ball occurred before the other foot landed in the lead position. If the ball is received after both feet have landed and are stationary, then either foot can pivot.

- The jump stop involves one count. Both feet contact the floor at the same time, with the body facing in the desired direction. The feet are spread for balance, and the center of gravity is lowered upon impact with the floor. Either foot may be the pivot if both feet are stationary or planted upon receipt of the ball.

Pivoting

Players with the ball use a pivot to align themselves with the basket or to protect the ball from defensive players. The pivot foot is the static foot around which the body rotates. The player chooses the pivot foot when both feet are on the floor and the ball is received. Using the passing pattern, students practice receiving the ball and pivoting right or left prior to releasing the ball to a teammate (see figure 5.4). Be specific about which pivot foot you expect students to use, and have them switch feet to allow them to become comfortable and proficient with either pivot foot.

There are two basic types of pivots: the forward pivot (stepping forward with the free foot) and the reverse pivot (stepping backward with the free foot). Students will progress through several variations:

- Jump stop forward-pivot right: Students land on both feet when they reach their corner and perform a 180-degree forward pivot on their right foot to face the center of the grid before rotating spots. This pivot initiates an offensive move toward the goal.

- Jump stop backward-pivot right: Students land on both feet when they reach their corner and perform a 180-degree backward pivot on their right foot to face the center of the grid before rotating spots. This pivot is used in Pick and Roll (see page 138).

- Jump stop forward-pivot left: Use the same movement as in the forward-pivot right but pivot with the left foot.

- Jump stop backward-pivot left: Use the same movement as in the backward-pivot right but pivot with the left foot.

With a Ball

Using the same movement described in moving to open space without a ball, one of the corner positions has possession of a ball and passes the ball to the person moving to the vacant spot. The passer waits until the receiver has performed the pivot and rotation to face the middle, with hands up and eyes on the passer.

The type of pass will depend on the sport; basketball uses different passes than soccer, football, or hockey. Regardless of the sport, be sure to allocate time for students to master each pass. For example, here are guidelines for a basketball bounce pass:

- Students bounce the ball past a defensive player who has arms up to a teammate cutting to the basket, or they pass inside to a post player.

FIGURE 5.4 Passing pattern.

- With two hands on the ball, students step forward in the direction of the pass and follow through with the fingers. The ball should contact the floor two-thirds of the way from the passer to the receiver.

Variations: Follow the same guidelines using a stride stop. Passers must time their pass for the receiver to catch the ball in midstride, plant the landing foot after the catch, and move the other foot to the lead. Receivers must concentrate on stopping forward motion with the lead foot and not moving the planted foot after reception. The planted foot is the only foot that can pivot.

Defenders

Once students begin to understand the concept of moving to an open space and watching their offensive teammates, they are ready for a defender.

Place students in groups of four, one group in each grid. One student is the defender. The three remaining offensive players must complete three passes without being intercepted or deflected by the defender, following these rules:

- The defender must stay at least 3 feet (1 meter) from the player who has possession of the ball.
- The player with the ball can only hold the ball for 3 seconds.
- At least one player must move to an open spot; however, the player with the ball can opt to pass the ball to either player.

Players rotate into the defensive position when they have completed three passes or three attempts.

Passing Strategies

Passes are often stolen when the passer looks directly at the receiver before passing, allowing the defense to anticipate the pass. Players must learn to disguise their passes through the ball fake, the eye fake, and the shot fake. The purpose is to freeze opponents or make them move in the wrong direction.

- **Ball fake:** Players extend the arms as though they are about to make a pass in one direction and shift their weight in that direction. They then quickly draw the ball back and step in a different direction as they pass the ball.
- **Eye fake:** Players stride forward toward the defender with their eyes in one direction while passing in another direction.
- **Shot fake:** This fake is similar to the ball fake, except that instead of faking a pass, players fake a shot, then bring the ball down and pass.

Grid Activity 2: Leading the Passer

In this activity, students progress to moving to an open space with a ball. The passer must lead the runner, passing the ball slightly in front of the runner. Remember to focus on the passing zones and 45-degree angles. The more aggressive the play, the larger the grid.

Without Defenders

Students can practice in pairs or with 3, 4, or 5 players. Successful catches are the most important thing. Students progress through the following skills:

- Passing to a moving target
- Moving and passing to a stationary target
- Moving and passing to a moving target

With Defenders

Establish groups that have one more offensive player than defenders (for example, three offensive players against two defenders, or five offensive players against four defenders). Every player must stay at least 3 feet (1 meter) away from each other. This prevents fouling and encourages offensive players to spread out and use the space.

Start by having offensive players complete three passes. Then an offensive player and defensive player rotate until all players within the grid have rotated between offense and defense. Progress to having offensive players attempt to move downfield and execute a complete pass across an end zone. If a defender deflects or assumes possession of the object, the offensive team starts again from that point on the field. The offensive team makes three attempts to score a goal. Once the team has scored a goal or made three attempts, the students rotate positions.

Grid Activity 3: Moving Without the Ball

As students learn to develop offensive and defensive strategies, they must also learn how to move without the ball to gain an offensive or defensive advantage. The following skills are essential for team play.

Fake Movements

Students can gain an offensive advantage by using fakes. Have them practice using head fakes, stutter steps, and leans to lose a defensive player to receive a ball. Students progress through the following skills:

- Receive a ball after making a V cut (moving in one direction and stopping with the lead foot to push off in another direction).
- Receive a ball from a person outside of the grid after making a move to get free.
- Fake in one direction and then move to the opposite direction, receiving a ball from a partner.

Next, assign four students to a grid. Players pair off to form two teams, and one team assumes possession of the ball. One player from the other team is the defensive player. The player with the ball must try to successfully complete a pass to his teammate. The teammate must perform a fake, such as jab step left and go right, to free herself from the defensive player and receive the pass. The passer must anticipate and lead the passer, using the passing lanes to successfully complete the pass (see figure 5.5). If the passer completes the pass, the other defender quickly assumes the defender position and play continues. If the defender intercepts the pass, he must pass the ball to his teammate and report to the opposite corner to receive a pass. The player who threw the intercepted pass becomes the new defender (see figure 5.6).

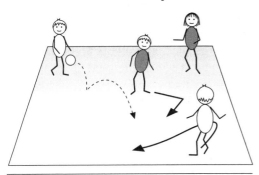

FIGURE 5.5 Fake movements: Pass is completed.

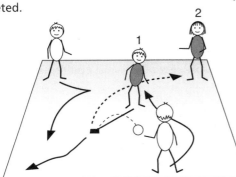

In this situation, the white team attempted to pass but gray player 1 intercepted. Gray 1 passes to gray 2 and goes to the vacant corner. The white passer becomes the defender and play resumes with gray on offense and white on defense.

FIGURE 5.6 Fake movements: Pass is intercepted.

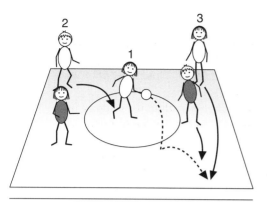

FIGURE 5.7 Post pivot.

Post Pivot

Students learn how to position themselves against a defender to gain offensive positioning. With quick passing, an offensive player can receive the ball even with an advantage of only a few inches. Students who are executing the pass will realize that a student doesn't need to be completely open to receive a pass, they just need the advantage of those few inches. Here students learn how to lead the receiver.

Set up three offensive players with one in the center of the grid. The offensive player in the center (the post) is not allowed to move but can only pivot on her right or left foot. She must attempt to pass the ball to one of her teammates. The goal is for the offensive team to complete three passes (see figure 5.7).

If the pass is completed, the other offensive player goes to the center to receive the pass. That player assumes the post position. The previous post player is now on offense, dodging with her teammate to receive a pass.

Next, students try to complete three passes in a row. If the ball is intercepted, the ball returns to the post to try again. Once the offensive team completes three passes, the teams switch roles. One member of the offensive team remains on offense the entire time.

Pick and Roll

Students learn how to free teammates from a close defender. For the pick and roll, students must be placed in groups of at least three, with one person in possession of the ball. The player with the ball is waiting for a teammate to gain offensive advantage over the defenders. There are times when individual fakes are not effective and a teammate must assist another by blocking the path of a defender to slow him down, allowing the teammate to gain offensive advantage. To accomplish this, teammate Gray 1 in figure 5.8 approaches defender White 2 to set a pick, a jump stop near the shoulder of White 2.

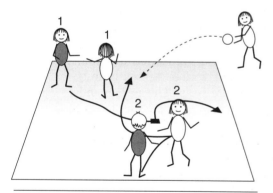

FIGURE 5.8 Pick and roll.

It's important to remind students when setting a pick to establish a wide stance on landing. Also, once a pick has been established, the offensive player setting the pick is not allowed to move. Gray 2 fakes away from the pick then runs toward Gray 1, brushing shoulders (the pick) to set himself free to receive the pass from the inbounder. Once Gray 1 has set the pick, she pivots and opens to the inbounder for another option to receive the pass. The player with the ball now has two options, the person who just gained an offensive advantage from his defender and the player who rolled from the pick. Gray 1 must remember to pivot in the direction that places her defender on her back as she opens to the ball. Gray 2 continues on offense until he has received the pass. Once received, Gray 2 passes back to the inbounder, and offense and defense switch roles. No lob passing is allowed.

Grid Activity 4: Playing Defense

Once students gain their offensive skills, it is important for them to learn defensive skills as well. Here students will learn how to anticipate movement by focusing on the core of the offensive player, keeping their hands in the passing lanes, and communicating with their teammates.

With the Ball

The term *passing lanes* is used in two contexts. The first is the path the ball travels in from one player to another. Ideally, this path is not directly from the core or abdomen of one student to another, because this type of path is easy to intercept. If you can imagine a person surrounded by a square that extends about 2 feet (61 centimeters) beyond him, the passing lanes would be the corners of that square. The other use of *passing lanes* would be the three imaginary lanes, like a bowling alley, that extend the length of a playing field or court.

Students at this point have practiced spreading the field to fully utilize the offensive options on the court or field and to maximize the passing lanes to an offensive player—leading the passer, extending the receiving grid of a player, pushing the corners, and so on. Students can progress to passing lanes while using the same drills as described previously, such as the pivot, post play, V cuts, and so on. Defensive players must keep their hands or implements in the passing lanes of their receiver. If the object is being thrown, the hands must be placed in the passing lanes. If the object is rolled on the ground, as in hockey or soccer, the defense must block those lanes with their stick or be ready to use their feet to block the path of the ball. The key to good defense is to always know where your opponent is and have a sense of where the other offensive players are located. A common mistake on defense is to lose sight of the player you are defending to see what the person with the ball is doing. Once the defender loses sight of her player, she is susceptible to fakes and picks.

When two defenders face three offensive players moving toward the goal, the defenders form a tandem (see figure 5.9). The front player moves vertically while the back player moves horizontally. The first player's objective is to stop the forward movement of the ball down the center lane. The second player's objective is to stop the opponents in the side lanes from passing, shooting, or driving to the goal.

The point player (the first person to meet the offense with the ball—Gray 1, in figure 5.9) is responsible for the center lane while the other defensive player is responsible for protecting the outer lanes. An effective tandem defense is able to protect the three lanes even if there is a three-on-two offensive advantage (figure 5.10).

In lane protection, the two defensive players work to thwart forward movement by assuming the responsibility of defending the three lanes; the point defensive player always assumes primary responsibility of the center lane while the other defender protects the sides. A very important skill for the point player to master when "off the ball" (meaning the ball has left the center lane and the point player has dropped down the center) is to keep the hands in the passing lanes to prevent a pass from side lane to side lane. The goal is to force the offense to pass to the center to get to the other side. This allows time for the back defender to resume the position and for more teammates to come and defend the goal.

You can add other rules to these activities, such as after passing, the player with the ball must move in the opposite direction from the pass before returning (give and go).

FIGURE 5.9 Tandem defense.

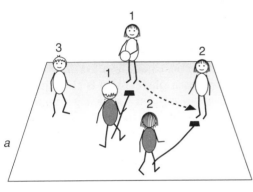

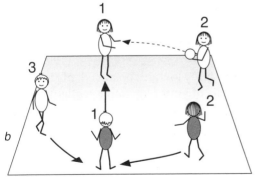

FIGURE 5.10 The offense has a three-on-two advantage over the defense: *(a)* The point player on defense forces a pass to a side lane, which the back defender covers; *(b)* White 2 is unable to advance and passes back to the center, giving Gray 2 time to return to position.

Without the Ball

Using the same setup as in the tandem defense drill, have the offensive players apply the principles they used in previous grid activities like give and go, post play, pick and roll, V cuts, and any other strategies for moving without the ball. You can also have an extra defender come to the aid of the two-person defense after two or three offensive passes, and play can continue three-on-three.

Use of the Field

Once students know and can perform the basic offensive and defensive principles, they will be more successful in a game situation.

Offensive Principles

- Spread the defense by maximizing the full playing area. Use zones or lanes.
- If possible, use matchups to gain an advantage on a defensive player's weakness with an offensive player's strength (e.g., quickness, height, strength, endurance).
- Use fakes and vary patterns to find open spaces.
- Use offensive moves like the pick and roll or give and go to create an opening.
- Lead the pass toward a teammate.
- Pass to the receiver's passing grid.
- Use 45-degree angles.
- Passing the ball is quicker than running the ball; however, if defenders are sagging (i.e., the passer finds there is no one defending her) to anticipate the pass, run the ball.

Defensive Principles

- Decide as a team whether you are going to defend an area or a person. Be creative! A combination of both may be necessary if one or two players are dominating play.
- Determine the best matchup for your team. If the offense has a player who is their primary offensive weapon, you can assign your best defensive player or two to defend the dominant offensive player and have the remaining players defend an area or concentrate on preventing forward motion of the ball.
- Keep your eyes on the torso of offensive players who threaten to move or who are moving and watch the eyes if they are stationary and preparing to pass or shoot; don't be fooled by fakes.
- Keep your body low and balanced, place weight on the balls of your feet, and stay light.
- Keep hands in the passing lanes of a receiver.
- Communicate with teammates about any exposed players or areas.
- Switch roles as needed.

Inbounding the Ball With Defense

Place students into groups of seven, with four on offense and three on defense. Play begins by one offensive player inbounding the ball to teammates within the grid. Offensive players can use a spread formation (figure 5.11a) or a line formation (figure 5.11b).

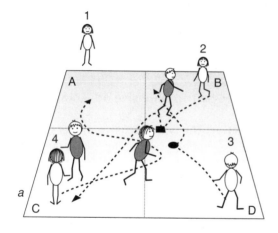

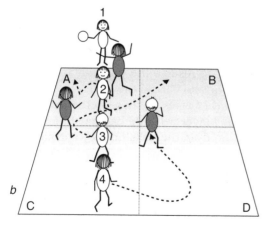

FIGURE 5.11 Inbounding (a) with a spread formation and (b) with a line formation.

Once the pass is successful, player 1 enters the grid, and the offense must complete five passes within the grid while the defense tries to intercept or deflect the pass. The offense can move freely within the playing area but can only receive a pass from another grid. Each completed sequence of five passes equals 1 point. The offensive team tries to earn 3 points. Offensive and defensive players switch after five inbound passes. Each sequence begins with one of the offensive teammates inbounding the ball from outside the grid.

This drill can be used with soccer, basketball, rugby, or hockey.

Three-on-Three

Although most people tend to think of three-on-three basketball, there are many advantages to teaching, practicing, and reinforcing skills using three-on-three games with football, hockey, soccer, and other team sports.

- Apply the rule of play (see page 133).
- If possible, use sidelines or end zones as goals instead of a small goal area in order to encourage success.
- The goal of the offense is to cross the end zone. The defense must try to prevent forward movement.
- The offense must try to cross the end zone with five or more passes.
- If the offense or defense is successful in crossing the end zone or preventing a score, players switch roles.

Grid Activity 5: Moving With the Ball

Students begin to practice basic offensive strategies against defensive players in a small playing area using the drills mentioned on pages 135 to 136 ("With a Ball"). Students must be comfortable with movement patterns before they can practice them while manipulating an object.

Game Strategy

You can apply the following strategies to soccer, rugby, football, ultimate Frisbee, or any game in which offensive players toss an object to one another.

- Mark a field with four corners that is the size of a small soccer field.
- Assign 4 to 6 players per team.
- Players must pass the object to their teammates and make a catch or receive a pass across the end line into the end zone to score a point.
- Once an offensive player receives a pass in the end zone, the player drops the ball or object. The other team immediately takes possession and play resumes from that spot.
- Any incomplete toss or intercepted pass changes possession from offense to defense, as well as direction of play.
- Students are not allowed to run with a tossed object and must make a pass within 3 seconds of possession. If students are playing hockey or rugby, they are allowed to take three steps before passing the ball to another player.
- Defenders must stay at least 3 feet (1 meter) away from any member in possession of the ball or object.

Summary of Grids

Grids isolate specific skills required for team sports such as football, hockey, soccer, team handball, and basketball so that students can develop their skills in settings that become more and more challenging. It's important to create activities and space that allow students to practice those skills and implement offensive and defensive strategies. Grids allow for the understanding and application of basic offensive and defensive strategies and foster communication and teamwork.

Unit 2: Gladiator Games

Gladiator games focus on the components of fitness and sport skills. Students are partnered with other students of similar size and skill. They move from station to station to participate in a series of activities that test endurance, agility, balance, and strength. These activities also help them understand principles of movement, including center of gravity, coordination, strategy, and power. As students gain experience with movement skills, they realize that it's not always the strongest who dominates a game or contest; rather, the person who is able to think and respond quickly to situations will most likely prevail.

Safety tip: In some activities like Dog Bone, Sumo Master, and Back to Back, it is critical that students are partnered with other students of similar size, strength, and skill. For students' enjoyment of the activity and to prevent potential injury or domination by one student over another, be vigilant of how students are participating in the activities. Stop play if students are unsafe.

Table 5.1 lists each activity. It shows the number of stations to set up, the total number of students who can participate at those stations, the skills involved, and the equipment needed.

Table 5.1　Gladiator Games Stations

Activity	Component	Equipment
1. Dog Bone: 3 stations, 6 players	Balance, agility	3 dog bones; white paint, or powder or chalk on grass
2. Rope Jousting: 3 stations, 6 players	Balance, agility	6 wooden pedestals, 3 15-foot (4.5-meter) ropes
3. Sumo Master: 2 stations, 4 players	Balance, power	4 Belly Bumpers; 4 protective helmets; white paint, or powder or chalk on grass
4. Hold 'Em Back: 2 stations, 4 players	Strength, power, speed	3 mats, 1 stopwatch
5. Battling Combats: 3 stations, 6 players	Balance, coordination	6 tires, 6 Combats or pillows
6. Push-Up Pull: 3 stations, 6 players	Speed, strength	Chalk, white paint, or rope on grass
7. Ball Wrestling: 3 stations, 6 players	Strength	3 medicine balls
8. Back to Back: 3 stations, 6 players	Power	Chalk or white paint
9. Flag Grab: 3 stations, 6 players	Coordination, agility	3 mats, 6 flag belts and flags
10. Towel Tug: 3 stations, 6 players	Power	3 towels; 6 cones; white paint, or powder or chalk on grass
11. No-Rope Tug: 3 stations, 6 players	Balance, agility	Chalk or white paint
12. Leg Wrestling: 2 stations, 6 players	Coordination, agility	1-2 mats
13. Breakthrough: 3 stations, 6 players	Power, agility, coordination	3 flag belts; 6 flags; white paint, or powder or chalk on grass
14. Power Ball: 2 stations, 8 players	Power, speed, agility, coordination	4 trash cans; 18 Eurofoam balls; white paint, or powder or chalk on grass

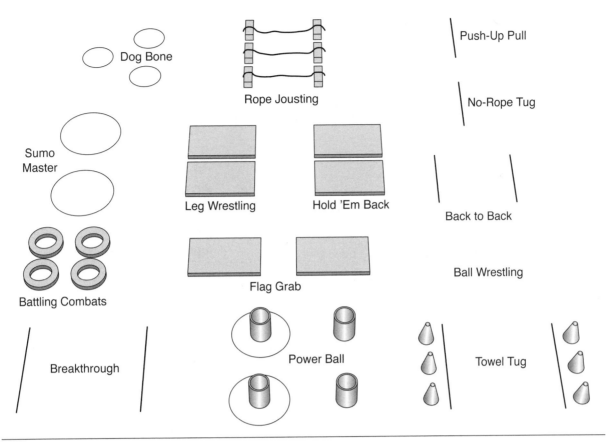

FIGURE 5.12 Gladiator games setup.

Figure 5.12 shows a sample layout for setting up the stations in an athletic field or gymnasium. In an indoor facility, mats are essential where their use is indicated. As you set up the stations, consider flow and spacing. Make sure there is sufficient space between stations to avoid incidental contact between students.

Each station will have a task card describing the activities students are expected to perform. Students move freely from station to station but are required to complete all tasks at a station. If a station is full, students can move to an available station and return to complete any station they may have missed.

To see a video of the gladiator games in action, visit the California Middle School Physical Education Workshop Web site at www.cmspew.org.

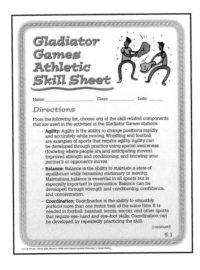

Instructional Sequence

1. Review the athletic skill sheet with students and ensure they are familiar with those skills (agility, balance, coordination, power, and speed). (See reproducible 5.1, "Gladiator Games Athletic Skill Sheet," on the CD-ROM.)

2. Provide an orientation with special emphasis on safety for each activity.

3. Help students select a partner of similar size and skill.

4. Hand out the athletic skill sheet to students so that they complete it as an assessment after participating in each activity.

5. Monitor student participation, ensuring safety.

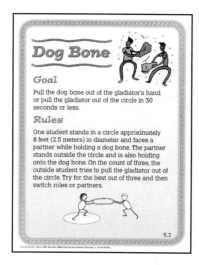

Dog Bone

One student stands in a circle approximately 8 feet (2.5 meters) in diameter and faces the other student while holding a dog bone. The other student stands outside the circle and is also holding onto the dog bone. On the count of three, the outside student tries to pull the gladiator out of the circle. (See reproducible 5.2, "Dog Bone," on the CD-ROM.)

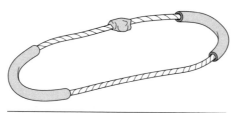

The dog bone can be a constructed using a 4-foot (1.2-meter) rope and two 8-inch (20-centimeter) garden hoses (see figure 5.13). The rope is pushed through the two pieces of hose and then the ends are tied using a double fisherman's knot. Place duct tape around the knot.

FIGURE 5.13 Dog bone.

Rope Jousting

Each partner stands approximately 8 feet (2.5 meters) apart on a 2- by 4-inch (5- by 10-centimeter) board that's 2 feet (61 centimeters) long. A 15-foot (4.5-meter) rope lies between the two blocks of wood. Players pick up their end of the rope. On the count of three, they try to unbalance each other by manipulating the rope so that the other person falls off the board. The match ends when one player loses the rope or falls off the board. (See reproducible 5.3, "Rope Jousting," on the CD-ROM.)

Sumo Master

Two students place Belly Bumpers around their waists and stand in a circle that is approximately 15 feet (4.5 meters) in diameter. They start with their Belly Bumpers touching and, on the count of three, attempt to push each other out of the circle. Students are not allowed to slam into their opponent. (See reproducible 5.4, "Sumo Master," on the CD-ROM.)

Belly Bumpers can be purchased through an equipment catalog (Gopher Sport, www.gophersport.com). Students must wear a protective helmet when performing this task, such as a Bell multisport helmet, also available from Gopher.

Hold 'Em Back

One student is the racer and removes her shoes and kneels on a mat. The other student begins at the end of the mat, grabbing one ankle of the racer. The racer tries to crawl to the other end of the mat while the opponent tries to keep the racer from moving forward by holding her ankle. Safety precaution: Racers are not allowed to kick back. (See reproducible 5.5, "Hold 'Em Back," on the CD-ROM.)

Battling Combats

Two students stand on tires, facing each other. On the count of three, they try to knock each other off balance and off the tire by hitting each other with Combats. (See reproducible 5.6, "Battling Combats," on the CD-ROM.)

Combats are long, foam-filled cylinders approximately 3 feet (1 meter) in length. Pillows could also be used for this activity.

Push-Up Pull

Two students get into a push-up position, facing each other, with their hands placed on a line between them. On the starting signal, each student attempts to make the other stop holding the push-up position by using one hand to push or pull their partner off balance. Students score a point if their opponent drops to one knee or falls out of the push-up position. They try for the best out of three and then challenge another person. (See reproducible 5.7, "Push-Up Pull," on the CD-ROM.)

Ball Wrestling

Two students grab a large medicine ball. One student holds the top and bottom of the ball and the other student holds its sides. On the count of three, the students try to snatch the ball away from each other. (See reproducible 5.8, "Ball Wrestling," on the CD-ROM.)

Back to Back

In the center of the area between two end lines that are spaced approximately 16 feet (5 meters) apart, two students stand back to back with their elbows interlocked. On the count of three, they try to walk forward toward their end zones. They provide resistance to each other since they are striving toward opposite ends. (See reproducible 5.9, "Back to Back," on the CD-ROM.)

Flag Grab

On a mat, students face each other on their hands and knees. Both students have a flag belt with a flag draped on the back of their waist. On the count of three, they try to pull out each other's flag. Students must remain on their hands and knees. (See reproducible 5.10, "Flag Grab," on the CD-ROM.)

Towel Tug

In the center of the area between two end zones that are spaced 16 feet (5 meters) apart, partners stand back to back in between the end lines, each holding one end of the towel. On the count of three, they try to walk forward and cross their end line without letting go of the towel. The activity ends when one student knocks down the cone that is standing behind the end line. (See reproducible 5.11, "Towel Tug," on the CD-ROM.)

No-Rope Tug

Two students face each other across a line and grab each other's hand (as if they were shaking hands) or wrist. On the count of three, they try to pull each other across the line. (See reproducible 5.12, "No-Rope Tug," on the CD-ROM.)

Leg Wrestling

Partners face each other on a mat, sitting down. While keeping the palms of both hands on the mat, they try to push each other off the mat using their hips and body. Students may change the position of their hands on the mat, but they may not use their hands to push or grab. The match ends when any part of the opponent's body comes off the mat or if students push or grab with their hands. Student must not kick each other. (See reproducible 5.13, "Leg Wrestling," on the CD-ROM.)

Breakthrough

Two students, an attacker and a defender, stand at opposite end lines of an area that is approximately 20 by 40 feet (6 by 12 meters). The defender wears a flag belt with two attached flags. On the count of three, the defender runs across the area and tries to cross the other end line without losing either flag. At the same time, the attacker tries to pull off one or both of the flags. The attacker may not tackle the defender! The defender scores 2 points for crossing the end line with at least one flag still in place, and the attacker scores 1 point for each flag pulled. (See reproducible 5.14, "Breakthrough," on the CD-ROM.)

Power Ball

This game requires four students and counts as two stations. Set up an empty trash can in a circle that is 8 feet (2.5 meters) in diameter. Set up a second can full of 7-inch (18-centimeter) Eurofoam balls behind an end line. The offensive team (two students) tries to score by taking balls one at a time out of the full can and tossing them in the empty can. The defensive team (two students) tries to block their shots and prevent them from scoring.

No students are allowed within the circle around the target can. If the ball is intercepted, the offense must retrieve the ball and start out of bounds to initiate play. If a ball touches the ground, it's out of play. In addition, students must follow the rule of play (see page 133).

After playing for 2 minutes, the offensive team moves to a new station and the defenders become the new offensive team against two new students entering the station. (See reproducible 5.15, "Power Ball," on the CD-ROM.)

Unit 3: Rhythm and Dance

This unit is a perfect setting for self-expression, but it's also the unit where students tend to experience the most stress. Most students enjoy music and rhythms, but many are afraid to dance in front of their peers for fear of looking foolish. Fortunately, MOOMBA creates an environment where students feel safe enough to take risks, and you can create a series of experiences that will help students gain confidence in a variety of rhythmic forms, from simple to more complex.

All of the activities in this unit are led by you. First, you should introduce rhythm by starting with baby steps. Although some students will be proficient in dance and movement, it's still necessary to begin with small steps so that all students can keep rhythm with the beat. To challenge the entire class and keep them engaged in the activity, keep the sequence interesting and fun.

Introduction to Beat

Sit in a circle. In front of each person are two plastic cups, one for the right hand and one for the left. Students should not touch the cups until you instruct them to do so. When the music begins, hit and clap the cups in time to the beat, and the students will do the same, following your actions.

You can beat the 4/4 rhythms listed here. It's best to start off with 60 to 80 beats per minute, like a heartbeat.

- Lift the cups and hit them against the floor to the beat.
- Bang the cups down for two beats and clap cups for two beats.
- Bang the cups down for three beats and clap cups for one beat.

Begin to use different configurations, such as placing a cup on your elbow, knee, chin, or nose for each count. When students are confident and following closely, have the circle pass cups. On the third beat, students pass one cup to the person on their right, and on the fourth beat, they recover their cup and begin the sequence again. This can be tricky since students need to understand mirroring, or doing the opposite of what they see when looking at you.

Introduction to Movement Steps

This section presents four lessons that introduce movement steps where all students can experience success: Paper Dance, Tinikling, Jump Rope, and Crash.

The Paper Dance is fun for students when you are having fun with it as well. You must be the focus of the activity—if all eyes are on you, then students are not watching each other. Students experience safety when they are captivated by the teacher.

In the Tinikling activity, students work in teams of four to demonstrate proficiency in six basic steps: the jump in and out, toe touch, walk-through, crossover, straddle, and scissors. The students focus on specific dance moves and on the clapping of the dancing sticks. The heightened level of concentration required to perform the tasks helps students become less self-conscious.

The Jump Rope lesson requires more complex movement skills since students are integrating movement with a moving object. Coordination and teamwork are necessary for students to perform a routine. The progression of rhythm and dance activities helps students to build the confidence and skills to create their own routine.

The Crash lesson introduces students to the components of dance, rhythm, syncopation, movement in space, vertical levels such as high and low, and movement or pathways on the floor. Students work in teams of six to eight to make a new sound by creating a performance that includes the components of dance.

Paper Dance

Lead the students through a series of movements manipulating a piece of paper. The students' eyes are on you so that they can mimic your movements, and therefore they are not paying attention to others attempting to accomplish a movement. Play music and use the rhythm to cue movements.

Here is a series of possible steps, but you can get creative and make your own.

1. March in place while passing the paper from left to right palms.
2. Pass the paper around your waist while marching in place.
3. Flap the paper up and down in front of your body.
4. Toss the paper in the air and catch it with both hands.
5. Pass the paper between your legs in a figure eight.
6. Crumble the paper in a ball while marching in place.
7. Bounce the paper on your knee and catch it with both hands.
8. Toss the paper over your shoulder and catch it with both hands while spinning around.
9. Throw the paper high and clap hands one time before catching it.
10. Throw the paper high and clap hands two times before catching it.
11. Throw the paper high and clap hands three times before catching it.
12. Throw the paper high and clap hands four times before catching it.
13. Straighten the paper and hold it against your chest.
14. Walk in a circle while keeping the paper on your chest with no hands.
15. Finally, crumble the paper again and toss it in the trash can.

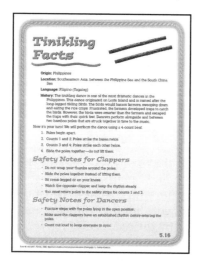

Tinikling

Tinikling is a wonderful first step in students developing an original group routine. The steps are basic enough for everyone, and the clapping poles add a dramatic element to the routines. As you introduce tinikling to your students, share the cultural history of the dance. (See reproducible 5.16, "Tinikling Facts," on the CD-ROM.) The handout not only gives a brief background of the dance but also reminds students of the safety precautions to use as clappers and tips for developing a successful routine.

The traditional Filipino tinikling dance is done in 3/4 time. However, teaching the dance using 4/4 time is easier for students to grasp. Additionally, it's easy to find popular music that fits the 4/4 tempo.

An excellent teaching strategy I use is to show students a video of a student performance that was exemplary. In the video, students used the steps taught in the introductory lesson, and the dance was creative, interesting, and choreographed in a manner so that all students were involved. Using student performance as an example encourages students not only to do their best, but it also gives them a clear example of what you as an instructor are looking for. I spend time with students after the video demonstration to review the grade sheet and ask students questions about the performance they just watched:

- Did they meet the requirements of the lesson?
- Explain how or what they did.

You will need two 6-foot (2-meter) PVC pipes or bamboo poles and two 2- by 4-inch (5- by 10-centimeter) clapper bases that are 3 feet (1 meter) long and marked with paint or tape (see figure 5.14). If you are using wooden clapper bases, wrap them in duct tape. This will prevent the pieces from scratching the floor, prevent slippage, and keep the wood from splintering. A different-colored tape can serve as the clapper marker.

Place students in groups of four. Each group has two clappers and two dancers. Students must be trained on proper use of equipment, as well as setup and takedown. Emphasize these safety rules for clappers:

- Do not wrap fingers around the poles.
- Slide the poles to meet each other—do not lift them.
- Stay in rhythm and watch the other clapper and the dancers.
- Move the poles between the marker points.

Students perform the dance moves described next. Clappers bang the poles twice on the markers on counts 1 and 2, and they slide the poles together twice on counts 3 and 4.

Jump In and Out

Both feet begin between the poles. Jump twice to the beat on counts 1 and 2 and jump outside the poles with both feet on counts 3 and 4. See figure 5.15.

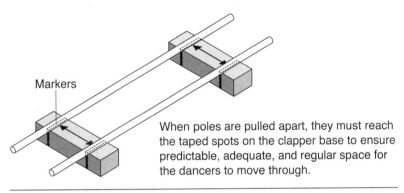

Markers

When poles are pulled apart, they must reach the taped spots on the clapper base to ensure predictable, adequate, and regular space for the dancers to move through.

FIGURE 5.14 Tinikling setup.

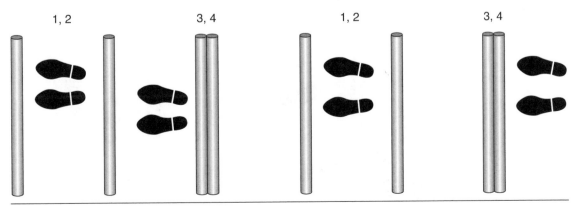

1, 2   3, 4   1, 2   3, 4

FIGURE 5.15 Jump in and out.

Toe Touch

Place weight on the foot outside the tinikling poles. With the inside foot, touch the toe twice between the poles on counts 1 and 2. See figure 5.16.

Walk-Through

On counts 1 and 2, place the lead foot between the poles and follow with the second foot. The lead foot leaves the center on count 2 and the back foot lifts on count 3. See figure 5.17.

Crossover

The crossover is similar to a walk-through, but the feet enter facing the inner pole and the legs cross over each other, as in a grapevine, through the poles. First the inside foot enters between the poles at a 45-degree angle on count 1, and then the outside foot crosses over the lead leg and is placed between the poles on count 2. On count 3, the lead leg crosses behind the other foot and plants outside the pole with the other foot immediately following. See figure 5.18.

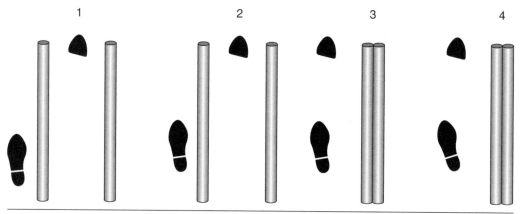

FIGURE 5.16 Toe touch.

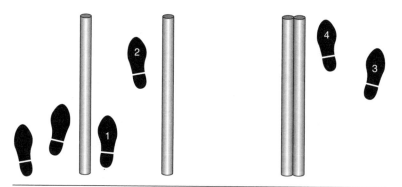

FIGURE 5.17 Walk-through.

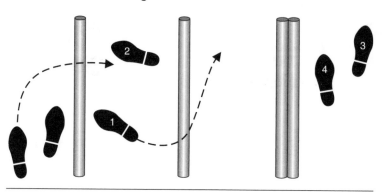

FIGURE 5.18 Crossover.

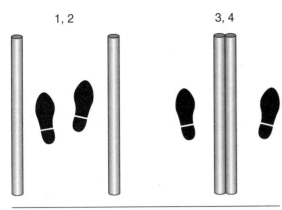

FIGURE 5.19 Straddle.

Straddle

Both feet start between the poles facing a clapper. On counts 1 and 2, both feet jump between the poles. On counts 3 and 4, both feet spread and jump outside the poles so that they're straddling the poles. See figure 5.19.

Scissors

Both feet start between the poles, facing one side. On counts 1 and 2, both feet jump between the poles. On counts 3 and 4, one foot moves forward and outside the facing pole while the other foot strides back behind the back pole. Both feet return for the next four counts, but this time alternate feet on the third and fourth counts. See figure 5.20.

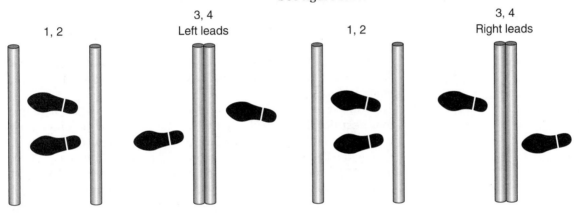

Scissors alternate feet on next sequence of counts 3 and 4.

FIGURE 5.20 Scissors.

Developing a Routine

Once students have basic mastery of the clappers and the six dance moves, they can prepare a routine. Students must include in their routine

1. all steps at least once,
2. transitions so that all members are tinikling (no student should remain a clapper for the entire routine), and
3. interesting variations on a step or incorporation of team moves.

When students understand what you expect in their routine, they get in groups of four and prepare an original routine. The CD-ROM includes a copy of the assessment sheet and routine planning guide for students to use while they prepare their dance. The example in reproducible 5.18 uses abbreviations for tinikling steps—for example, "CO" stands for "crossover," and "SS" stands for "scissors." (See reproducibles 5.17, "Tinikling Self-Assessment," and 5.18, "Tinikling Routine Planning Guide," on the CD-ROM.)

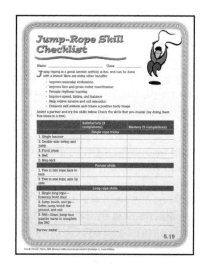

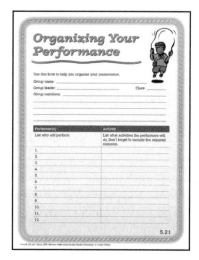

An effective way to improve student performance is to present a video of students performing a routine that scored well on the assessment. After the students watch the video, they review the assessment sheet and answer these questions:

- What score would you give the team based on the assessment provided?
- What did the team do well to earn the score?
- What is important to include in your routine?

Jump Rope

This is an interesting unit since many students have experience with jump rope but rarely in an organized setting. It is more complex than tinikling because of the unpredictable speed of the turners. However, jump rope is an excellent way to introduce tricks and teamwork in the curriculum while providing an incredible workout.

If students have progressed through the previous rhythm and dance activities, they should now be able to work independently with a worksheet to complete tasks as outlined in the jump-rope checklist. Students are expected to work through the checklist and complete as many tasks as possible.

Before starting, make sure students know how to select a jump rope that best fits them. Students hold a jump rope by the ends in either hand and stand on the center. Students pull up on the ends of the jump rope while keeping their elbows pressed against their body. The ends of the jump rope should reach slightly above the belly button.

Students will begin with individual tasks, then move on to partner and group activities. Encourage students to have fun and to try different skills and tricks. Included on the CD-ROM are checklists students can use to chart their progress. (See reproducibles 5.19, "Jump-Rope Skill Checklist," 5.20, "Jump-Rope Performance Checklist," and 5.21, "Organizing Your Performance.") Eventually, students are challenged to put together a jump-rope routine with a group of other students.

Crash

The Rhythm and Dance unit culminates with the Crash lesson. Students choose from a variety of equipment, including trash cans, trash-can lids, sticks, poles, brooms, paint cans, hula hoops, basketballs, or anything that can make a noise and is safe for students to manipulate. After choosing equipment, students are placed in groups of 6 to 12. Each group must compose a musical piece with choreography that lasts from 90 seconds to 2 minutes. Within each group, a student leader records the dance routine on the performance planning guide. As you prepare your students for the performance, hand out the Crash Rubric so they know how their routine will be graded. (See reproducible 5.22, "Crash Rubric: How Will I Be Graded?" on the CD-ROM.) Each routine must include the following elements:

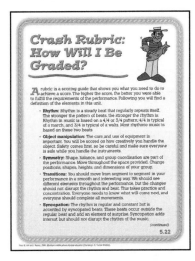

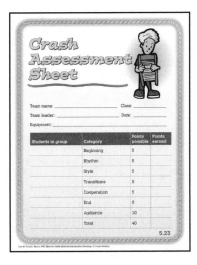

- **Rhythm:** Rhythm is a beat that regularly repeats itself and is steady; the stronger the pattern of beats, the stronger the rhythm. Rhythm in music is often based on a 4/4 or 3/4 pattern. 4/4 is typical of a march, and 3/4 is typical of a waltz. Most rhythmic music is based on these two beats.

- **Object manipulation:** The care and use of equipment is important, so you should score how creatively students handle objects. Safety comes first, so they must be careful and make sure everyone is safe while they handle the instruments.

- **Symmetry:** Shape, balance, and group coordination are part of the performance. Students move throughout the space provided, changing positions, shapes, heights, and dimensions of the group.

- **Transitions:** Students should move from segment to segment in the performance in a smooth and interesting way. The performance should include different elements, but the rhythm and beat should not be disrupted by the changes. This takes practice and concentration. Everyone needs to know what will come next, and everyone should complete all movements.

- **Syncopation:** The rhythm is regular and constant but is accented by syncopated beats. These beats occur outside the regular beat and add an element of surprise. Syncopation adds interest but should not disrupt the rhythm of the music.

Each group works independently to choreograph a routine. Students take approximately 3 to 5 days to establish their routine and prepare for their performance. Providing more time than this usually results in students losing focus and going off task.

Give groups an assessment sheet so that they know what you are looking for in an exemplary routine. (See reproducible 5.23, "Crash Assessment Sheet," on the CD-ROM.) In addition, consider showing a video of routines performed by other students so they can see what they need to do. After watching the video, ask the following questions:

- What grade would you give this group?
- Why would you give that grade?
- Look at your assessment sheet. What were they graded on? How did they meet the expectations of the assessment sheet? Be specific.
- What am I looking for in an exemplary piece of work?
- What are you going to be sure to include in your routine?

The Dance Checklist is provided as a basic form to be used as an assessment tool for student performances. (See reproducible 5.24 on the CD-ROM.) Students will then know what is expected for their team performance for each routine.

Promoting Your Program

> "**H**ope sees the invisible, feels the intangible, and achieves the impossible."
>
> —*Anonymous*

ost physical educators feel uncomfortable promoting their work. However, we need partners to make a positive, long-lasting impact on the lives of our students, and that should drive us to overcome any difficulty we might have in seeking support for our work. A good start is to create a message to communicate to parents, staff, and students. It's much easier to promote your work when you've created a mission statement that everyone can rally behind. Examples of common themes and their mission statements that everyone can support include the following:

- **Success for all students.** We believe that all students experience success. Therefore, we focus on challenge by choice and provide a wide variety of challenges that develop skills to push students to become more proficient.

- **A lifetime of health and wellness.** We believe that the most important skill we can teach our children is to be healthy and participate in activities that support a lifetime of health. Therefore, we integrate a nutritional wellness component within our curriculum. In addition, we incorporate a wide range of lifetime recreational activities such as swimming, hiking, and orienteering.

- **Creating leaders for a global society.** We believe in developing students who know how to work cooperatively with others, resolve differences, and take responsibility for their actions. Therefore, we stress group initiatives and train them in peer mediation.

- **Creating students of character.** We believe that physical education includes character development. Therefore, we incorporate citizenship within the curriculum. We teach students about character development and recognize them for outstanding behavior, and we stress citizenship in all activities.

Whatever theme your department chooses as the best one to promote your program, that theme will drive the units and learning emphasis of the curriculum.

Address the Three Circles of Influence

Educators can achieve excellence when they address the three circles of influence in their work: self, department, and school and community (figure 6.1). The circles overlap and support each other, requiring communication that seeks understanding and integration. It's critical for department staff to be emotionally and intellectually committed to the success of the program. All staff members must be committed to the goals and vision of the department and live that commitment each day. Every action and interaction must be through the lens of what you believe.

Circle 1: Self

Make a professional commitment to examine your instructional practices as reflected in student engagement and performance. Participate in professional development and organizations to push yourself to higher levels of proficiency. Join your state AAHPERD chapter. Attend your state, national, or regional physical education conference. Examine the national teaching standards for physical education and reflect on your practices.

Circle 2: Department

Establish a curriculum that offers a wide range of activities, meets students at their level, and challenges them in appropriate ways. Make sure expectations for student performance are clearly stated, including examples of outstanding performance. Students will gain the knowledge and skills to work independently as well as cooperatively.

Circle 3: School and Community

The physical education curriculum should support school-wide learning outcomes and recognize students for outstanding achievement. Strive for parental support in developing lifestyle changes toward health and wellness.

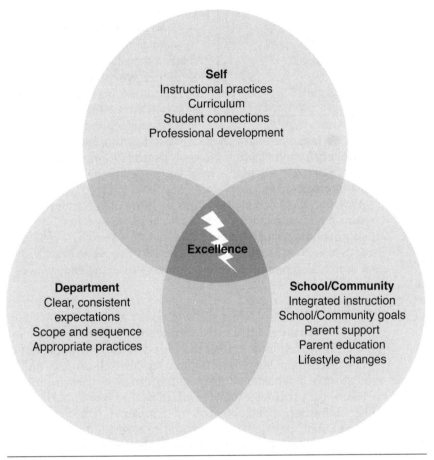

FIGURE 6.1 Three circles of influence.

Build the Curriculum

To create a quality physical education program, it's necessary to reflect on what that kind of program looks like and what experiences students need in order to achieve that goal. As discussed in chapter 1, physical educators need to understand best practices in physical education, examine national standards, and perform a self-study using the criteria outlined by NASPE (www.aahperd.org/NASPE/). The Education World Web site (www.education-world.com) lists physical education content standards for every state.

Scope and Sequence in Action

First, look at the state and national standards for a good curriculum. Then ask yourself these questions:

- What are students expected to learn?
- What are appropriate activities for each grade level and each student?

Creating appropriate activities requires planning and constant evaluation of student performance. Are all students becoming proficient in the skills you expect them to learn? If not, how can you either revise the instruction or provide learning experiences that adequately prepare them for learning the new skills? The Scope and Sequence Worksheet helps you plan backward to ensure the curriculum (what is taught) is a learning sequence designed to meet your learning outcomes (what you expect students to learn and do). (See reproducible 6.1, "Scope and Sequence Worksheet," on the CD-ROM.)

In addition, it's important to build professional relationships with other teachers in order to develop a curriculum that maximizes student and teacher performance. Visit other teachers known for their effective teaching strategies. Be specific in what area you are looking for information on, such as transitions, time on task, or assessments. These outside perspectives help reveal your effectiveness in a manner that is professionally safe but challenging.

After you have established your working plan for improvement, begin defining what actions staff and students need to do in order to reflect your philosophy, and establish clear expectations for behavior. Your message should be reflected in the selection of units, how they are taught, and what is assessed. Everyone must know why physical education is a critical component in every student's learning experience.

Essential Units

As you build a curriculum, think about what essential units you could introduce at each grade level. Such units stress the foundation of physical education as well as lead to optimal development of psychomotor skills, self-esteem, and social skills. All physical educators in a department are required to cover the essential units.

Figure 6.2 provides examples of units that one department may consider essential. Other units have been selected to complement the curriculum and enhance student participation. Your department might or might not agree that these items are essential; the point is that each department must decide what should be taught in each grade and how that work will continue each year to strengthen skills.

Essential units	Component
Adventure games and group initiatives	Social skills, critical thinking, leadership skills, problem solving, communication
Circus tricks	Psychomotor development, balance, coordination, self-esteem, agility, strength, exploration of physics, confidence building
Beginning jump rope	Coordination, balance, agility, cardiorespiratory fitness, cooperation, teamwork, leadership skills
Beginning juggling	Eye–hand coordination, perseverance, patience

FIGURE 6.2 Sample essential units for sixth grade.

Spread the Word

The final step in promoting your program is developing a strategy to get the message out. Videos, back-to-school nights, open houses, family fitness nights, newsletters, press releases, grants, special events, and recognition programs are all avenues to inform parents, staff, and the community about your program. Some of these strategies are discussed next.

Videos

Tape student performances or activities and share them with students, parents, and school staff. This lets people know what you're doing. In addition, showing the best performances can enhance students' engagement. For example, before beginning a dance unit, show a student performance from the previous year and then discuss why it was outstanding. You can also show a video of students in action at a parent night so parents can see their child participating in a program that supports all students.

Back-to-School Nights

Prepare a brochure and presentation that outline your program and stress the purpose and philosophy of physical education. Outline the units that will be taught and focus on the skills students will learn.

Family Fitness Nights

Invite parents to come with their children to a family fitness night at the school. Engage the parents in the activities that students are experiencing in your program. Use group initiatives and have the students be the student leaders of the night. The student leaders facilitate the activities for the parents. Parents not only see middle school students assuming leadership roles but also experience them being responsible, respectful, and caring. Play a noncompetitive game where students partner with their parents. Share with parents the value of physical fitness, wellness, social skills, and team building. Help them become partners in your work. Provide parents with activities they can do at home with their families. Encourage them to create time within the week to play and exercise together.

Your students can help you prepare materials to promote your fitness program.

Special Events

Schedule evenings within the school calendar to sponsor events for community participation. Make contacts with your local high schools, sporting franchises, or health clubs and see what events they can sponsor or provide for your families. Partner with local doctors, nutritionists, or the school nurse to sponsor a health fair for families to learn more about health and nutrition.

Recognition Programs

Recognition programs highlight students who demonstrate important behaviors. For example, if you strongly believe that students should learn to work cooperatively with others, then the entire department should focus on social skills, peer mediation, conflict resolution, and team building. Develop a common language that students hear from teacher to teacher, year to year. They will begin to realize that what their teachers are saying is important. If you believe physical education is about fitness and wellness, then build a program that recognizes achievement in that area. Parents, staff, students, and anyone who comes into contact with your program will be able to see what you stand for as a department because it lives through student behavior and actions.

Find Support

Establish support for your program by communicating expectations for student behavior to administrators, other department members, parents, and the community.

- Meet with the administrative and counseling staff before the school year and make sure all parties are aware of your expectations.
- Know what the consequences will be if students are unable to meet those expectations, and be prepared for interventions to support changes in student behavior.
- At the beginning of the year, send home a letter that provides an orientation to your program.
- Sponsor a special event, such as a family fitness night, to communicate the purpose of your program and to help parents get to know you and support your intentions.
- Visit other programs that have been recognized as outstanding by professional organizations in order to gain new perspectives and to see how things can be done more effectively.

Bringing It All Together

1. Develop a quality physical education program.
   - National standards
   - State framework
   - Appropriate practices
   - Meeting the needs of all students
2. Create clear expectations for students and staff.
   - Collective will to achieve excellence
   - Professional development
   - Behavioral standards
   - Goals for achievement
3. Promote your program.
   - Videos
   - Articles
   - Special events
   - Recognition of achievement

MOOMBA is about maximizing yourself as a teacher. The better you are at what you do, the better the experience for students will be. As educators, we can create physical education experiences that promote health, happiness, and wellness. It is time we all responded with a concerted effort, but it requires us not only to stay focused on the goal of quality for all but also to respond to the needs of one. It also requires that we engage in conversations with colleagues, parents, and members of our community to support our work. It also requires us to have the courage to examine our own practices and measure our effectiveness based on the performance of our students. Our young people cannot afford to have us deflect the responsibility. We not only have to believe we can make a difference, but we must also act as if we should.

What are the obstacles that keep us from reaching our students? We must assume the responsibility of what occurs in the classroom and constantly find ways to engage and reengage students in incorporating movement into their lives. MOOMBA is not allowing our attitudes to get in the way of student success. MOOMBA is our ability to be open to new ways of approaching a situation, student, concept, or bias that promote positive attitudes toward self and others and allow us to grow personally and professionally. In MOOMBA, there is always an eagerness to learn, share, grow, and apply.

Our hope is that through *Maximum Middle School Physical Education* you have learned what we have learned over the years. Students learn best when they are in an environment that is safe and respectful. Students thrive when they are encouraged to be challenged and supported when they fail. Students want to take responsibility for their learning, and they love to experiment and discover on their own. And, most of all, we all love to have fun. So have fun trying the ideas presented in this book, and may the MOOMBA philosophy serve you well!

References and Resources

Graham, G., S. Holt/Hale, and M. Parker. (2004). *Children moving: A reflective approach to teaching physical education.* 6th ed. Mountain View, CA: Mayfield.

Hichwa, J. (1998). *Right fielders are people too: An inclusive approach to teaching middle school physical education.* Champaign, IL: Human Kinetics.

Mohnsen, B. (2003). *Teaching middle school physical education: A standards-based approach for grades 5-8.* 2nd ed. Champaign, IL: Human Kinetics.

National Association for Sport and Physical Education (NASPE). (1998). *Physical education, program improvement and self-study guide.* Reston, VA: NASPE.

NASPE. (2004). *Moving into the future: National standards for physical education.* 2nd ed. Reston, VA: NASPE.

Sizer, T. (1996). *Horace's hope: What works for the American high school.* Boston: Houghton Mifflin.

Zakrajsek, D., L. Carnes, and F. Pettigrew Jr. (2003). *Quality lesson plans for secondary physical education.* 2nd ed. Champaign, IL: Human Kinetics.

Professional Development

California Middle School Physical Education Workshop: Summer workshops focusing on best practices in middle school physical education. www.cmspew.org

National Board for Professional Teaching Standards: Exemplary teaching standards in physical education that meet National Board Teaching Certification. www.nbpts.org

National Association for Sport and Physical Education: NASPE seeks to enhance knowledge and professional practice in sport and physical activity through scientific study and dissemination of research-based and experiential knowledge to members and the public. www.aahperd.org/NASPE

Curriculum Development

Christy Lane Productions: A collection of music videos, books, and CDs for dance. www.christylane.com

PE Central: A site for physical educators to glean the latest ideas and lesson plans. www.pecentral.org

PE Links 4 U: Internet resource for physical educators. www.pelinks4u.org

Project Adventure: Seeks to develop responsible individuals, productive organizations, and sustainable communities through experiential learning. www.pa.org

Equipment and Supplies

Sportime: 800-283-5700; www.sportime.com

US Games: 800-327-0484; www.us-games.com

About the Authors

Mary Hirt, BA, has been named the Middle School Physical Education Teacher of the Year for California (2002), the Southwest (2003), and the nation (National Association for Sport & Physical Education, 2003). She is a Nike Go PE master trainer and a SPARK master trainer (SPARK creates, implements, and evaluates programs that promote lifelong wellness). In her 20 years as a teacher, Ms. Hirt has presented at numerous conferences, including the National Physical Education Conference. During her spare time she volunteers at a boxer rescue organization in Los Angeles, training dogs and preparing them for adoption. She also enjoys rock climbing.

Irene Ramos, MEd, has over 21 years of experience in education, including 16 years as an administrator with an emphasis in student support services. She has presented at several state and regional conferences on maximizing and promoting student achievement. A member of the Association of California School Administrators, Ms. Ramos received her MEd from UCLA in 1990. She enjoys hiking, jogging, and bike riding in her leisure time.

How to Use the CD-ROM

The *Maximum Middle School Physical Education* CD-ROM includes over 150 worksheets, forms, assessments, signs, station instructions, and other resources to use with students. These resources are grouped into seven files, one for the introduction to the book and one for each of the chapters. Each resource is identified by title and number, and thumbnails in the book help you find the right resource for each activity.

System Requirements

You can use this CD-ROM on either a Windows®-based PC or a Macintosh computer.

Windows

- IBM PC compatible with Pentium® processor
- Windows® 98/2000/XP/Vista
- Adobe Reader® 8.0
- 4x CD-ROM drive

Macintosh

- Power Mac® recommended
- System 10.4 or higher
- Adobe Reader®
- 4x CD-ROM drive

User Instructions

Windows

1. Insert the *Maximum Middle School Physical Education* CD-ROM. (Note: The CD-ROM must be present in the drive at all times.)
2. Select the "My Computer" icon from the desktop.
3. Select the CD-ROM drive.
4. Open the file you wish to view. See the "Start.pdf" file for a list of the contents.

Macintosh

1. Insert the *Maximum Middle School Physical Education* CD-ROM. (Note: The CD-ROM must be present in the drive at all times.)
2. Double-click the CD icon located on the desktop.
3. Open the file you wish to view. See the "Start.pdf" file for a list of the contents.

For customer support, contact Technical Support:

Phone: 217-351-5076 Monday through Friday (excluding holidays) between 7:00 a.m. and 7:00 p.m. (CST).

Fax: 217-351-2674

E-mail: support@hkusa.com